Yes, You Can Wear That

YES, YOU CAN WEAR THAT

HOW TO LOOK AND FEEL FIERCE AT ANY SIZE

ABBY HOY

TILLER PRESS

New York   London   Toronto   Sydney   New Delhi

TILLER PRESS

An Imprint of Simon & Schuster, Inc.
1230 Avenue of the Americas
New York, NY 10020

First Tiller Press hardcover edition November 2021

TILLER PRESS and colophon are registered trademarks of Simon & Schuster, Inc.

For information about special discounts for bulk purchases, please contact
Simon & Schuster Special Sales at 1-866-506-1949 or business@simonandschuster.com.

The Simon & Schuster Speakers Bureau can bring authors to your live event. For more
information or to book an event, contact the Simon & Schuster Speakers Bureau at
1-866-248-3049 or visit our website at www.simonspeakers.com.

Interior design by Matt Ryan
Photos on page vi, viii, 6, 8, 12, 15, 21, 22, 24, 31, 32, 36, 39, 40, 45, 46, 50, 56, 63, 65,
66, 70, 88, 96, 101, 105, 106, 124, 132, 135, 138, 146 by Source Creative House
Photos on page 74, 83 by Dave Gerz

Manufactured in China

10 9 8 7 6 5 4 3 2 1

Library of Congress Cataloging-in-Publication Data

Names: Hoy, Abby, author.
Title: Yes, you can wear that : how to look and feel fierce at any size / by Abby Hoy.
Description: First Tiller Press hardcover edition. | New York : Tiller Press, 2021. |
Identifiers: LCCN 2021005853 (print) | LCCN 2021005854 (ebook) | ISBN 9781982155582
| ISBN 9781982155605 (ebook)
Subjects: LCSH: Fashion.
Classification: LCC TT507.H69 2021 (print) | LCC TT507 (ebook) | DDC 746.9/2—dc23
LC record available at https://lccn.loc.gov/2021005853
LC ebook record available at https://lccn.loc.gov/2021005854

ISBN 978-1-9821-5558-2
ISBN 978-1-9821-5560-5 (ebook)

To my baby nephew, Emmett,
who had the same due date as my book.
He came early and I was late.

To my parents, my twin pillars,
as Amy Sherman-Palladino would say,
without whom I could not stand.

To my dear friends
Cassie and Hannah, who held my hand
through the whole process.

To Afa, the first person
who ever believed in me.

And last (but much like Gretl,
most important): my darling husband,
Preston. I love you and I like you.
The biggest understatement in this
book is that I couldn't have done
it without you.

Contents

SUGAR,
EVERYT
(+ CHE

SPICE & IN NICE
MICAL X)

DURING MY SENIOR YEAR OF HIGH SCHOOL, I had a civics teacher whom I absolutely adored. (Anyone catch that obscure *It Takes Two* reference? A true Olsen twins classic.) Mr. Mack was smart and funny, but most important, he was just a great educator. I learned so much in his class—way more than what was on the syllabus. On our very first day, he had all the students enter and didn't say a word as we sat down. After a few silent moments of him starring at us, he told us to stand up. At that point, we all thought he was going to put us in assigned seats, like just about every other teacher. But he didn't. He told us to sit down, stand up again, sit down again, stand, sit, stand, sit . . . This went on for what seemed like a long time, but really was probably only five minutes.

In true *Dead Poets Society* fashion, young Mr. Mack did this until someone (spoiler alert: it was me) finally said out loud, "I'm sorry, Mr. Mack, but why are we doing this?"

He pointed his finger at me and, channeling his inner Robin Williams as John Keating, said sternly, "Good. You should question authority if it feels weird to you. Now sit down wherever you want and let's get started." And from that moment, this class chatterbox was pumped for Mr. Mack's class. Questioning authority and staying as absolutely close to the line without crossing it when it came to rules definitely spoke to my inner rebel (or . . . at least as much of a rebel as a Goody Two-shoes like me could ever be).

Mr. Mack's class was just . . . different. He refused to give us multiple-choice tests because he believed that those types of exams didn't prove we had learned anything, just how good we were at memorizing facts and spitting them back out. So all his tests were open-ended—the only instructions were that we could write however we wanted in order to best convey that we had actually absorbed something.

"Because not everyone thinks in neat, tidy paragraphs," he told us. "List some facts, draw a cartoon, write a few sentences, whatever! Anything goes, as long as you prove that you learned something."

I obviously loved these directions. For as long as I can remember, I've always been looking for a way to push the limit. I would walk right up to the edge of a syllabus of what was "allowed" and actively work to make something innovative and memorable. For an entire semester of civics, I drew cartoon panels to discuss civil rights issues and resolutions. My crowning achievement: an epic *Roe v. Wade* cartoon. (Seriously—it was really awesome.)

I got an A in the class.

I also learned something really important about myself: I am not good at writing neat and tidy paragraphs. I don't like them. My brain doesn't think in neat and tidy paragraphs.

Why on earth would I start my book with neat and tidy paragraphs?

So without further ado, here's a list of some important things about me and why you should keep reading, even if you're a neat-and-tidy-paragraphs type of person.

My name is Abby Hoy. Hi!

I am currently in my late twenties.

I "pay the bills" as a social media influencer and content creator. I've been doing this in some capacity since 2014.

You might know me better as ThePennyDarling on social media!

I started my blog in 2016 and quit my day job before the end of 2017.

My husband, Preston, and I have been married since 2018. We met, got engaged, and got married in a community theatre in a park. He's the absolute best cinnamon roll; he's simply good to the core.

I am an adult theatre kid. Take from that what you will.

I once had an alien encounter in Roswell, New Mexico.

The first poem I remember writing was in fourth grade, shortly after 9/11, as I started using writing to deal with emotions I didn't understand. I still have a copy.

I have a bachelor's degree in communications, and it has mostly made me insufferable to my loved ones because whenever we fight, I ask people to reframe things in "I statements."

I am a *Saturday Night Live* mega fan. I memorize stats about each person on the show (like original characters vs. impressions) the way some people keep stats on sports stars. During the COVID-19 lockdown, Preston and I watched twelve years' worth of *SNL* episodes.

For some reason, I cannot pronounce the word "sixth."

One of the things on my bucket list is to have a menu item named after me, so if you happen to be a restaurateur with a nameless dish, please keep me in mind.

I have an eight-pound morkie named Charlie. Preston and I adopted him from a rescue the day after our wedding. Charlie loves laps and is scared of potted plants. He is a very good boy.

I am the type of person who likes to dress my dog in themed outfits.

I cannot dance to save my life. I once won an award in an elementary school theatre production for having "two left feet."

I am open about my journey with depression, anxiety, and chronic pain. I'm pro-therapy, pro-meds, and pro–mental health treatment.

I have never met a print I didn't love. Polka dots? Absolutely. Stripes? Stripe it up, baby! Plaid? I'm plaid to wear it!

I'm a Gemini. My husband is a Virgo . . . if you're the astrology type.

I wrote the book you are reading right now, and that is WILD! The wildest part about that? It's a book that's mostly about fashion! (And other important things like loving yourself, saying "thank u, next" to the haters, and all that fun stuff.)

What's super crazy about this is that I used to NOT *do* fashion. If you look at pictures of me back in high school, I was wearing jeans and T-shirts. In college, I upgraded to wearing leggings and V-necks. At one point, I actually owned twelve of the same V-neck in different colors, exactly two skirts, and a single dress. I didn't own anything pink or anything containing ruffles, and absolutely nothing that even hinted at a rainbow. Hard to believe, I know.

I was lazy. I was in a hurry. I didn't care about my clothes. I was plus-size and there was one rack at the department store in town with tags up to an XXL. There were no plus-size stores. Plus-size "fashion" wasn't a thing. I had been resigned to not having choices when it came to shopping and was just grateful to have something to wear at all, let alone something fashionable.

I got my first job at a theatre two days after I graduated from college. When I asked what the dress code was, the answer was "business casual" (which, I learned later, was SO not true). As you can probably tell after hearing the extent of my wardrobe, this was an issue. Like, a major one.

I was scheduled to start the following Monday. As a recent college grad, I had next to no money, so I went to some local outlets and thrift stores, hoping to find something I could afford. And I scored HUGE. I bought five bottoms, eight tops, a coat, a dress, and a pair of shoes for under $60. It was an epic haul, honestly. I posted pictures of it on my Instagram and got an overwhelmingly positive response.

Now, when I say the feedback was overwhelmingly positive, I mean probably all of two friends commented and gushed that I had great style, asked if I'd go shopping with them, or complimented my new outfits. But I really loved that feeling!

So I started taking pictures of my outfits every single day in the mirrors of my first big-girl job. I bought new clothes at thrift stores and off clearance racks with carefully saved pennies. I experimented with print and pattern. I learned what felt good on my body. I figured out what made me feel good as a person. I trial-ed and error-ed the absolute heck out of my own style. My sense of style grew as I felt less and less limited by my plus-size body.

I worked at that theatre for a year and a half, until I was laid off. In that time, just through posting my outfits, I gained a few hundred followers on Instagram. When I was laid off, I felt lost. It was the first time since I had started working at age fifteen that I was unemployed. I had no plan. It took a toll on my mental health. Where was I going now?

I started taking more and more pictures—mostly from my parents' back porch—as a way to keep busy. Soon I tipped from 999 followers to the delightful 1,000 mark. I was growing, and fast.

A friend of mine from college, Afa, had experience working in influencer marketing and would sometimes text me random advice. She explained logistics, suggesting how to gain followers, how to monetize, how to market, and how to keep growing, and quickly became my biggest supporter and my best mentor. I listened to all her advice, and it worked. I remember that in one of my early outfit pictures, I wore a skirt right out of the package, and it looked incredibly wrinkled. I posted the picture and Afa texted, "If you ever post a picture with wrinkled clothes again, I'm gonna smack you in the head. Iron them, dummy." I laughed so hard at that, but she was absolutely right. Afa is still involved with *The Penny Darling* today, I haven't worn a wrinkled garment since, and I've learned to take her advice because she's usually right.

A few months later, while still gaining more followers, I was offered a temporary job, this time at an office. And honestly, this job was soul-suckingly dull. It wasn't challenging or creative or vibrant like my job at the theatre had been. I didn't fit into this culture of salads and quiet in the hallways—everyone just seemed so . . . basic. Worst of all? I didn't get any cell service in there. No texting, no social media scrolling, none of it! I was so bored.

After a month of absolutely dreading going to work, I decided I needed something to do to keep myself entertained. I started my blog *The Penny Darling*, mainly because I didn't need my phone to do it. I could toggle tabs and write all day long.

I wrote my blog posts during my downtime and between instant messaging meetings with people who were ten feet away from me. My following grew. I started upping my photography game to give myself the colorful-background aesthetic to match my over-the-top fashion and style. When the temp job ended, I kept blogging, and kept on at it when I landed another gig, this time at a university.

The job itself was much more fun and exciting, but the pay was terrible and the commute was long. The plus side of working at a university was that it allowed me my summers off. I decided that during my first summer off, I was going to scrimp and save and see if I could make any money on my blog without having to get another job. I hustled, and it paid off: That July, I got my first sponsored blog post. It wasn't enough to pay even one household bill, but I was ecstatic.

When summer ended and I went back to work, my position at the university had drastically changed—it was no longer fun or exciting, and there was no room to grow. I felt like I was going backward. I was constantly on edge, having panic attacks about events that had already happened. I knew it was no longer a place where I could grow.

I figured if I was going to be making only a few bucks more than minimum wage, I might as well shorten my commute and get a job in something far less stressful. I applied to a few retail jobs, a few nanny positions, really anything part-time to supplement my income so I could keep blogging. In this search, I met the Wilsons.

The Wilsons were an older, conservative religious couple with absolutely no sense of humor. In all my interactions with them, I never saw either of them smile or laugh. Mr. Wilson was leaving on a work trip for a few months and Mrs. Wilson had recently suffered an injury. They wanted me to come over for a few hours every day to heat up a meal, keep her company, and supervise her doing physical therapy in their pool. They were offering to pay seven dollars more an hour than my university job for the same hours per week and it was only a ten-minute commute. It was almost too perfect; plus, they offered me the job on the spot. Two days later, I gave notice at the university.

After the initial interview and job offer, I went back to the Wilsons' to go over some logistics. In that meeting, they asked me to take on some tasks that had very much not been part of the job description, chores that were pretty demeaning. I politely declined, saying that they had not hired me as a maid, but as a "personal assistant," and that I wasn't comfortable taking on these extra assignments. The tone in the room shifted. They seemed shocked that I said no. The meeting ended awkwardly.

Four days after that, I got an email from Mr. Wilson saying they no longer needed my services. I wrote back that this rendered me without a job at all, as I had given notice at the university. Despite his harsh demeanor, Mr. Wilson understood that this left me in a tough position, and mailed me a check for two months' severance for a job I never worked. It bought me time to grow, and eventually became the seed money for *The Penny Darling*. Mr. Wilson had become my unexpected, grumpy savior.

I moved a desk into my living room, bought a camera better than the one on my phone, and started plugging away. It felt like my entire life turned into one big cycle of trial and error. Setting up photo locations and modeling became an outlet of self-expression for me. As *The Penny Darling* grew, so did I, and so did my confidence.

I remember shortly after that, I interviewed a woman who had opened her own business for a post where I was talking to local shops in my hometown. I asked her what the best business advice she had ever gotten was. She told me, "Sometimes you leap, and the net appears." I started to tear up—her advice was so spot-on. So many times, I had taken leaps, only for the net to appear at the last minute. Her words still hold true to this day.

Right now, I'm taking way too big of a leap by writing a book. I started blogging as an escape from the mundane nuance of my post-college millennial life, and it ended up being so much more than that. I've come a long way over the past few years. I've learned a lot about myself. But I have a long way to go and continue to look forward to the person I am going to be.

So with this book, let's leap together. Leap into *being* more self-confident every day. Leap with your fashion and trends. Leap even when you feel like you're way too close to the bottom. The net will appear, I promise.

Let's leap together, cuties!

MUCH LIKE MARIA VON TRAPP, I HAVE CONFIDENCE

CONFIDENCE IS NOT A DESTINATION. It's a lifelong journey.

I didn't "get to be" so confident in my body. It's something I work on every day. I have moments where I'm tugging at shorts that I'm worried are too short. I have moments where I spend thirty minutes staring at my own chin and crying about it. I have moments where I feel like everyone at the gym is staring at my thick thighs.

But I work through it. Being confident doesn't mean you're not susceptible to negative feelings. Instead, it means your self-assurance is louder, your personality is bolder, and your self-love is bigger than the bad feelings more days than it's not. That's it.

Now, there's a big difference between your body confidence and your self-confidence, at least the way I see it. Most people think the way they feel about their body is what's holding them back from having self-confidence, but truly, it's having the latter that gives you the former. (Woof, say that five times fast, I dare you.) You need to have confidence in yourself before you can have confidence in your body.

My body? My body is easy for me to hate or love on any given day. My body image fluctuates with the seasons, with hormones, with the weather, with whatever. But certain days are memorable. I remember getting out of my shower one day, seeing my naked body in the mirror, and instead of pinching my love handles with disdain or feeling sad about my stretch marks, just feeling *exhausted*. Truly, genuinely exhausted.

I was just so tired of being unhappy with my body. I thought that if for just one day, I could not care about how my body looked or moved or jiggled, I would be happy. So that day I vowed to spend an entire twenty-four hours just being a person in a body. Not a fat person, not a scared person, just a person. I kept my head up. I took up space. It was weird and wild and wonderful.

Who was I worried wasn't going to like my body? No one around me was stuck with the damn thing like I was. I had better start liking it, I thought. It's all I was ever going to have. This realization hit me like a bolt of lightning.

After that day, I started waking up and thanking my body for what it could do for me. *Thank you, hands, for helping me send this text. Thank you, nose, for smelling the fresh-cut grass. Thank you, toes, for keeping me balanced. Thank you, ears, for letting me hear my dog sniffing to wake me up in the morning. Thank you, skin, for being freckled.* I did this every day until I didn't feel like I needed to anymore. Every once in a while, I still have to thank my body, but it's a lot less frequently these days.

People around me started to notice my change in attitude. Friends commented that there was something different about me, but they couldn't quite put their finger on it. But I could. I was walking taller and taking up space. It felt really good.

I had fun getting dressed and choosing clothes. Choosing an outfit became a positive part of my day. The fact that I had choices, plural, was so novel and exciting. I looked forward to getting dressed for things. I stopped dressing to "cover up" and instead wore clothes that made me feel good. I didn't care if my outfit violated some old fashion faux pas. I didn't care if some woman in the grocery store noticed the cellulite on my thighs. *I don't know that lady, and she has seventeen cans of creamed corn in her cart. Why would I care what SHE thinks? Also, who needs seventeen cans of creamed corn?*

Because truly, I didn't care about her opinion. She didn't know me. This took years of telling myself, *You don't care what they think,* about complete strangers before this lesson really took hold, before it became my default attitude. And some days I do still need to remind myself that my opinion of myself is the only one that matters. My self-confidence is still something that I work on every single day.

Even though developing self-confidence is no picnic, having body confidence is even trickier. Every day you have to tell yourself that you deserve to take up space; that you deserve to not have to hide; that you deserve to exist in the world without shame; that you deserve to like who you are, even if you have parts you don't like.

Even though I do it pretty regularly, I am super shy about shooting pictures in public. (I know you're thinking: *Weird career choice if that's the case, bro.* But here we are!) I hate to be watched or looked at. I get so nervous in photo shoots that I've been known to have panic attacks or start crying. Once, as I was posing for a Cinderella-themed Halloween photo, a huge group of European tourists trotted by, and I was so frustrated with how worked up and nervous that made me. (I live in my state's capital, and it actually does attract foreign tourists.) As I stood there, blushing and frustrated, I asked myself, *What do I care what these people think?* I was NEVER going to see them again! So I yelled to my husband (and main photographer), Preston, who was watching my growing embarrassment from farther down the steps of our state capitol building, "DO I EVEN CARE?!" and kicked one of my shoes off (for the Cinderella look, obviously). And guess what? The tourists cheered! It was the first and only time in my life I've had "Slay, queen!" yelled at me with a Swedish accent, but it's an experience I won't soon forget.

There have been countless times that I've gotten frustrated with myself for feeling self-conscious. In my experience, I'm usually annoyed at my own innate inability to do what other people do so easily: NOT CARE. And in order to not care, there's some stuff you have to unlearn.

Mythbustin' Free

At some point in your childhood, someone taught you some general "rules": how to dress, how to act, and just how exist in the world. You learned what your expectations should be and what you believe you deserve. I learned those things from my parents, while others may have learned them from a sibling, a grandparent, or a teacher.

And while we can learn a lot from older folks, unfortunately, times change, and what held true for one generation might not be applicable now. Also, as you age and grow and realize things, you learn new ways of thinking and develop new perspectives. You should do that—try to break down some of your learned habits or biases. A fun example: My husband, Preston, hates the Pittsburgh Steelers. But he isn't even a sports fan! We don't watch football. His rivalry is a learned behavior that he would be better off getting rid of. That behavior can go back in his bachelor box with the twin bed and beer posters.

Your negative biases about your body, or your thoughts on what you should and shouldn't wear? Well, those are learned, too. Which means you can unlearn them—and help other people unlearn them, too.

Now that I'm an adult, my mom will regularly call me and ask if she can wear something. The conversation usually goes something like this:

"Can I wear horizontal stripes?"

"Yes, Mom. You can wear that."

"What about skinny jeans?"

"Yes, you can wear that."

"What about yellow? Can I wear yellow?"

"Yup, that, too."

Unteach your mom things!

We have this type of exchange probably once a week. She loves texting me her #OOTD (outfit of the day) photos, with her rocking skinny jeans or a trend I've never seen her wear before (while serving NO face, making her look like a serial killer). I love that! I'm so happy my mom is starting to feel more comfortable and confident in her body. It's been such a fun transition to watch her get to a place where she feels more comfortable.

It's definitely a bit crazy that I have to unteach my mom all these lessons about fashion that she taught me. Growing up, she told me that "plus-size women don't wear horizontal stripes" and that we "don't wear bikinis." She reminisced about the first and only summer she felt she was "skinny enough" to wear a two-piece bathing suit. My mom was taught by her own mother that plus-size women always needed shapewear and girdles. Her mother put her on diets when she was in elementary school. My grandma wasn't shy about letting my mom know that her body was a work in progress, and that less is more when it comes to a woman's body. My mom wasn't shy about teaching me the same. In every decade and generation, this strong diet culture and beauty standard was upheld by some fad, whether it was corsets in the 1890s or medical-grade cocaine in the 1990s, in a way that almost feels timeless.

My wardrobe growing up reflected those ideas by containing no horizontal stripes or really any type of fun patterns. I had my first pair of shapewear by the time I was sixteen. I never even thought to question these ideas. They were as ingrained as taking off my shoes before I stepped on the carpet—something I did without thinking about it because it just . . . was. I didn't even know that I should challenge those ideas. For me, these ideas came from my mom. For her, it was her mom. For you, it could have been a father, a friend, a coach, anyone who was hypercritical of your body early in your life. If we, the (*Degrassi*) next generation, don't challenge these standards, we condemn a future generation to the same extreme body image issues and ingrained fatphobia we grew up with.

Before I could really challenge my ideas of what self-confidence looked like, I had to examine all the things I had been taught. It was the starting point of unlearning these myths. When I started really examining these ideas, I realized that my first idea to challenge them was: *You should build your wardrobe with things you love, not things you're "supposed" to have.*

The point is, times change, and wearing the clothes you want to wear shouldn't be radical. Liking your body and dressing it for function and fit should not be radical.

So let's talk about what you can and can't wear.

"I wish I could be as confident as you."

When I hear this, I am always reminded of this story.

I once had a coworker who always complimented my outfits, so I shared that I had a blog. She, like me, was plus-size, and noted that she was glad I was young and could pull off this "young, trendy stuff." She told me that she mostly stuck to wearing jeans and T-shirts from a big-box store. I told her there were SO many plus-size retailers these days. I pulled up close to ten websites to show her, but she just looked uncomfortable to even be discussing plus-size clothes.

After a few minutes of scrolling, she confided, "I wish I could be as confident as you. I used to be so thin and athletic, but two kids and twelve years later, and now I'm this size. I hate it. I have tried and failed so many different diets. I just can't be as confident as you."

This was tough to hear. I replied, "It's not that I'm super confident, it's just that the alternative is that I wake up every day and hate my body. And that doesn't really seem healthy." She kind of shrugged it off, and that's where the conversation ended.

This happened years ago, but I'm still thinking about it. I wanted to shout at her, "Don't you know it's OKAY to be fat now? We have options, girlfriend! You're allowed to be cute!" Or, "Who cares if you've gained weight?! Wear clothes that fit and feel good!"

But I didn't. I was worried I would offend her or cross a line. I was young and new to the company and worried I'd come on too strong. So I didn't say any of those things. Looking back, I really wish I had.

Whenever someone comments on a plus-size woman's self-confidence, there's a smidge of self-loathing behind it. It implies that you NEED to be confident to exist as a plus-size person who has some style and personality. And that's loaded with fatphobic implications. Do you tell every straight-size person that they're confident for wearing shorts? Probably not. Next time someone says they wish they could be as confident as you, tell them, shout it from the rooftops, and sing it to them: "YOU CAN!"

Final Thoughts

Your confidence can be rooted in your environment, but you're the flower. So bloom, baby! You can practice self-advocacy against fatphobia; you can rebel against your learned body biases!

It might take a while to get there, but you can. To start, every time you feel embarrassed or ashamed of yourself because of your body, ask yourself: *Who cares?* If the answer is "nobody," then nothing is wrong. If the answer is "I care for me," then you can work toward your goals. There is no normal.

You get to define what your normal looks like. You get to decide what your style looks like. Because that crop top or bright jumpsuit or those horizontal stripes?

Yes, you can wear that!

A Three-Letter Word

FAT IS A NEUTRAL WORD.

THAT IS ALL. Fat is a neutral word. It is not a synonym for "ugly." It assigns no value to your self-worth. You can't "feel" fat, you can only *have* fat. Let go of "fat" being an unflattering word. So many times in my life, I have had some form of the following conversation.

Me: I am fat.

Anyone: You're not fat, you're beautiful.

You can be fat AND beautiful. It's not an either/or type of situation. "Fat" is just a three-letter word. You can be fat and beautiful and sexy and valuable and cute and worthy of love and attention, all at the same time. Anyone who says otherwise is simply wrong.

POLKA DOT COM

LIKE MOST TEENAGE GIRLS, one time in high school, my best friend asked me to go to the mall with her. Obviously, it was a Saturday night. After all, where else could suburban fourteen-year-olds go to be mildly unsupervised? On this occasion, we headed to the nicer of the two malls in my town. When we got there, my best friend wanted to buy a new pair of jeans. We went into a trendy teen store that had a smell so pungent, you could almost taste their pumped-in store cologne all the way from the food court. But I didn't care. I loved picking stuff out with my best friend and styling her outfits. She was petite and had choices. So many choices—she could shop almost anywhere. There was only one store in the mall that even sold clothes in my size; it wasn't cute, and I was limited to whatever they had in stock. I usually went there with my mom. I never went clothing shopping for myself with a friend.

Back in this cologne-drenched teen store, my friend pulled the maximum number of garments one could take to try on. Keep in mind that she was a notoriously slow person, and this was before the days when everyone and their mom had a cell. So I had to stand outside the fitting room and wait for my (notoriously slow) bestie to try on eleven pairs of jeans. With nothing to stare at, I just stood there like a lunatic in my juniors plus-size jeans, holding nothing, and . . . waited.

I waited and waited. My self-consciousness left me continuing to scan the same four racks of semi-edgy graphic tees and pretending to browse. Every few minutes I would get a glimpse of my friend, but otherwise, I was desperately trying to disappear into the background. Somehow, we were the only two customers in there, so the twentysomething cashier was continually asking if she could help me with anything. After assuring her for the millionth time that I didn't need anything, she started folding sweaters at a table that had clearly been messed up by previous shoppers. At a loss for literally anything else to do, I went over, struck up a conversation, and started helping her fold the shirts.

I usually tell this story as a funny anecdote. When I told another plus-size friend, she grabbed my hands and exclaimed, "OMG, SAME!" and proceeded to tell me about a time she straightened up a rack of earrings while she waited for her straight-size friend to come out of a dressing room. Another friend told me she used to make excuses that she needed to stop in another store to pick something up. I once mentioned this anecdote on Instagram, and my inbox flooded with dozens of different versions of this story.

Even to this day, when I go to a mall with other people and stop at stores that have since extended their sizing, my straight-size friends don't notice that while the entire store caters to them, there might be only one or two racks with my size. Or when I ask if we can stop in a plus-size-exclusive store, these same friends drop that they've never even heard of that particular store. It's constantly disheartening.

So to avoid these types of experiences, I was early to the ordering-my-clothes-online game. I started online shopping in high school, which was unusual back in my day. (Oh my gosh, am I one thousand years old?) The choices were limited and bland. There was no colorful or quirky and accessibly priced clothing for my body type. Everything seemed like it was made to *hide* my body type. Luckily, by the time I graduated from college, plus sizes were expanding. More and more stores were extending their sizing, and more and more plus-exclusive shops were popping up, although almost exclusively online—which made me really good at online shopping.

Seriously, I am the Michael Jordan of online shopping. If internet shopping were an Olympic sport, I would at least medal every time. Seriously, try me. I can find almost anything that's for sale online. I've gotten so extremely good at it that I sometimes forget that people need to return things they bought online. I'm so often right about my online order that I basically never need to return things.

I think my crowning achievement of online shopping happened one night when I was having trouble sleeping. I kept flipping my phone on, scrolling, and then trying to fall asleep again. A few days later, a pair of pants showed up on my doorstep. I had apparently fallen victim to one-click ordering and had ordered some leggings while I was mostly asleep. I didn't even remember doing it. But they fit perfectly and I still own them—that's how good I am. Seriously, I'm looking for my casting agent to put me in the online shopping equivalent of *Space Jam*.

Sometimes followers on Instagram will ask me where I got my clothes. When I say the name of almost any online outlet, they've never heard of it! That absolutely blows my mind. We're in the 2020s, baby! I mean, Costco sells coffins online, so you can definitely find a dress to wear to your college roommate's wedding.

We're so far into the (*Zenon: Girl of the*) twenty-first century that you can even thrift shop online. You can shop small and local and sustainable online. There's no excuse not to be doing it!

Online Shopping Tips

For some, online shopping seems daunting, risky, and nothing more than a general hassle. As a millennial, I know that folks even a few years older than me can feel overwhelmed by online shopping. I know friends who fill up virtual carts that they never intend to purchase. There's just something scary about clicking that buy button. Never fear, friends! I promise it's not as daunting as it feels. Much like David, I will take the Hassel-off.

1. Know your measurements.

For goodness' sake, right this moment, buy yourself a sewing tape (one of those soft measuring tapes). I have a whole bunch of them floating around. Measure your bust and your waist (not sucked in) and write the measurements in a note on your phone. Most companies offer size charts, and being able to utilize them properly will continue to change your game.

2. Read the reviews.

Read the reviews. Let me say it again: Read the reviews. Read the five-star reviews AND the one-star reviews. On any clothing site, people can generally leave "fit" reviews, meaning they'll tell you if an item fits true to size (TTS) or whether it runs large/small, what the fabric feels like, if the hem is a little short, etc. Reviewers can usually post pictures as well, so you can see the clothing a little more IRL. I highly recommend reading reviews before buying.

3. Know the return policy.

The biggest downside to online shopping is returning. As a society, we're getting better at it, but it's still a big enough hassle to turn some people off online shopping altogether. Before you buy, double-check the site's return policy. Sometimes there's an additional charge for returning, sometimes items can only be returned in person, and some items can't be returned at all. Sometimes you can return online purchases in-store, which is always convenient. If you're a frequent Timmy (re)Turner, make sure you know the policy.

*PRO TIP: Choose which card you use wisely. It takes, like, seven million times longer for money to be returned to a debit card than to a credit card. Take it from my broke-college-kid experience.

4. Check materials/ care details.

You can usually find this information under the Materials tab online. Cotton and denim are durable and classic and will last forever. Satin, silk, leather, and cashmere are high quality but also high maintenance. Viscose rayon and polyester are both synthetic fibers and pose their own set of limitations. If something's made of a fabric you've never heard of before, look it up! Knowing what your clothes are made of will tell you if the fabric is breathable, if it's prone to wrinkles, what the general wear and tear on the garment will be, and its life expectancy. Your future self will thank you.

5. Think outside the browser.

Get creative! If you can't find what you're looking for with a quick search, change it up. You're not just limited to retail stores. Check secondhand resale sites and auction sites. Sometimes influencers or bloggers will run secondary Instagram pages selling nearly brand-new clothing as they cycle through their wardrobe. Heck, I have one! This is one of the hacks that make my friends think I can find anything.

6. Check out influencers!

Hi! Influencers are totally the new retail advertisers. We are literally paid to know the online trends first. Following people who have an aesthetic you really like will lead you to new stores, new styles, and new trends, and it can be cool to see those stores and styles on a body type that is similar to yours. I get probably twenty DMs a day just asking where I buy my clothes. Most influencers tag stores that they love shopping at, write reviews of any product you can think of, and style outfits from multiple retailers.

7. If you're not familiar with the company, double-check that it's not a scam.

If you find a designer dupe for a quarter of the price, you're likely going to get a quarter of the quality. There are tons of websites that rip images from more popular retailers and sell the "same" product, but you'll end up with a cheap mess if you even get the product at all. A quick search will return reviews, any scam alerts, and any fraud claims against the site. My rule of thumb: If it seems too good to be true, it probably is. Take this from a person who bought a $140 dress for $68 that never even showed up and read the reviews too late and was out $68 for not taking two seconds to verify.

8. Remember to allow time for shipping.

You can avoid many a fashion panic moment by allowing time for shipping. My anxiety brain makes me order really far ahead, but generally, plan on having any garment at least two weeks before the event you need it for, if possible. That gives you time for ordering, processing, or shipping delays, ironing, styling, and any other little thing you can think of. Plus, it'll save you the extra cost and stress of express shipping.

9. Find shipping deals.

If you look hard enough, you can find a shipping deal. Whether it's order minimums, signing up for an e-newsletter, or even a promo code, there's almost always a deal to be found somewhere. Sometimes it's cheaper to buy a pair of socks to hit a free-shipping threshold than to actually pay for shipping.

10. Get a browser extension.

For the love of widget, find a browser extension for coupons. You can add little buttons to your web browser that you can click in ANY promo code box at online checkout and it will run through every available discount for basically any store. I have saved close to two thousand dollars over the past three years by literally just clicking a button in my browser. So worth it. My favorite dollar saver is the extension Honey!

Final Thoughts

Shopping online has been an absolute savior for my style. It blows my mind on the regular how many options there are just waiting online.

I used to feel suffocated by my lack of choice when shopping in person, so I absolutely adore the feeling of being overwhelmed by the amount of choice online. Every day, more and more retailers are realizing that the market goes above a size 6 these days. In the past few years, two of my favorite aesthetic retailers expanded to plus sizes, and I was so pumped to see it happen.

If you're out there feeling like they don't make cute clothes in your size, I am happy to break it to you—you're wrong! I have a pink tutu, onesies, high heels, fishnets, tights, a closet full of pretty coats, comfortable and cute running sneakers, rompers, overalls, and a million other items I thought I would never be able to wear! And now? Yes! I can wear that! And in my size.

TULLE
THE
WORLD

1. Start changing your own narrative.

Yeah, judgy pants, I'm looking at you. That means you need to stop internally (or externally) judging others for dressing feminine. Embracing femininity includes not judging people who are already doing it.

2. Slow to glow!

Add a pink blouse, a rocking polka-dot blazer, some sequins or glitter, one piece at a time. It feels a little less scary when it's a gradual addition.

3. Pink isn't just a "girl" color.

Pink is a powerful and fun color. Stop gendering it at all! Men can wear pink! Women can wear pink! Nonbinary and gender-fluid friends can wear pink! We can ALL wear pink! Embrace the color pink as just that: a color, with no added meaning or insinuation attached to it.

4. Don't lose your professionalism.

Be sure you're still aligning with the company culture and dress code. If you work in a law office and you show up in a rainbow sequined suit, that isn't fitting the company culture, and I can almost guarantee it doesn't fly with the dress code. However, if you're working at a school or a day care or the front desk of a vet's office, you can definitely rock that dress or those scrubs covered in ponies. Check that vibe.

5. Confidence is key.

If you know what you're talking about, people will listen. It might just take them a few extra seconds to be truly "listening" if you're wearing a blouse with unicorns. Make them regret doubting you. Speak up!

6. Much like the cheese on *Schitt's Creek*, fold that color in.

Add it slowly (as mentioned on page 36), but make sure it feels right for you. Mix it with neutrals. Add pops of color via funky earrings. Carry a hot-pink briefcase. You don't need to transition your whole wardrobe to 100 percent femme—you can add just one femme piece at a time if that feels more comfortable.

7. The tailor Motel Kamzoil.

How do you think A-list celebs are out there making white T-shirts look sexy and feminine? A tailor. That's right, they tailor their clothes. Even more straightforward pieces (like blazers or trousers) can benefit from being tailored, and it's usually not too expensive. Tailoring a plain blouse or even black pants can add a feminine touch to something classic. If budget is a concern, do it slowly, over time, starting with the pieces in your wardrobe that you wear most often.

8. Femme is a state of mind.

We're so far into the twenty-first century now, gender is basically irrelevant. So remember that all these tips are not just for women! Anyone can add a touch of femininity to their wardrobe, if they want to. It's a personal expression, not a gender law.

9. Advocate out loud.

When Martha made that sly comment about my shoes, I responded with, "I didn't know my sandals made me worse at my job." Martha didn't say anything about my shoes again. Making a nonaccusatory statement like this helps normalize your "abnormal" fashion choices.

10. Start your own dang company.

Why wait? I can't say that deciding to leave my office job wasn't partially from struggling under the constraints of "the real world." I didn't like that I had to fit into a box, so I made my own box that I fit into perfectly. And I made dang sure that I was never going to need to follow a working dress code.

This is a bit of a dramatic response, but it was mine, and I am dramatic.

10½. If you're going to follow Warner to Harvard, make sure you get the partner offer.

Elle Woods taught us all too well. We all need to go through our "crying in a bunny costume" phase to get to our "winning the trial" phase.

Starting my own business, I wanted to be taken "seriously." I wanted to be listened to, respected, to feel like I was adding to a conversation. I wanted to expand my creative wingspan and make strides. I wanted to create things that had never before existed. Did I truly NEED a boring black pantsuit or shapeless baggy sacks to make any of those things happen? No! When I ditched the "serious" stigma and started expressing myself through my wardrobe at work, that's when *gestures vaguely* all of this started!

I take my mantra and general rule of thumb on being taken "seriously" from the iconic RuPaul, when they hosted *SNL*: "Baby, just have fun. And if you follow your heart and dare to be different and use all of the colors in the crayon box, who knows where you'll end up. If you're lucky, you just might find yourself hosting *Saturday Night Live*."

Hosting *SNL* might not be everyone's dream (like it's mine), but that advice is as sage, relevant, and magnificent as RuPaul.

Final Thoughts

Let me just say that louder for the people in the back: You can be a beauty queen in the streets and a freak in the spreadsheets! You can wear a pink blazer and be a true boss. You can carry a rainbow lunchbox, wear things tailored to fit a feminine shape (if that's your style!), and rock a professional scrunchie (Professional Scrunchie, new band name, I call it), all while killing it in your career.

An empty desk
is the sign of an
empty mind, so I
never mind that
mine's cluttered.

WHAT'S A MOTTO?

"Nothing. What's a-motto with you?"

—"HAKUNA MATATA"

I'VE NEVER BEEN ONE FOR MANTRAS OR INCANTATIONS. No shade to them, they've just never been for me. And as a half-assed rebel, I've never been one for rules that I couldn't at least bend. So I'll keep my intro short and share some of the mottos I dress by. Yes, I'm taking my lead from Timon and Pumbaa, and calling it a motto.

I never liked the idea of fashion "rules," because fashion is fast and fluid. It changes and ebbs, season to season, year to year, decade to decade, and never stops evolving. When I started my first day of kindergarten, I wore a row of butterfly clips, and on my fifteenth birthday, I was wearing blue eyeliner on my top *and* bottom eyelids. Hell, I can remember when jelly bracelets got banned from middle school, and multilevel marketing leggings took over my college years. Trends in fashion are changing constantly.

How can you possibly follow rules that change basically day to day? Instead of trying to memorize arbitrary rules, I have a few fashion mottos that I stand by. These aren't hard-and-fast rules, but they do serve as good guidelines.

If you love, buy it in every color.

Seriously. If you find a top or a dress or a style of underpants that you love, buy it in every color. At one point, I had seven of the same dress in varying colors. The store likely won't sell that cut forever, so make sure you stock up. Because, if you love it, you'll utilize it.

If it comes in your size, you can wear it.

Don't be out here saying that you can't wear horizontal stripes or that you can't wear bikinis. No one but you is saying you can't wear it. As long as it fits you, you CAN wear it.

While we're on size . . .

. . . it's arbitrary and meaningless, so don't let it hold you captive. Don't get stuck on the idea that you're any one size. If a bigger size fits better, buy that. Clothing sizes differ wildly in every country, at every store, and for every garment. Wear what fits, and don't get hung up on the number. I have clothing in my closet ranging from size medium to 6X, and they all fit the same.

Don't buy clothes that aren't comfortable. Period.

Not for your wedding. Not for special events. Not for dates. Not for anything. Repeat after me: Not. For. Anything. Truly, no matter how pretty it is, you'll never look pretty in something if you feel uncomfortable—you'll just look uncomfortable.

Highlight, don't hide.

I spent so many years dressing to cover my visible belly outline (VBO). I hated that little pouch, so I wore only long tunics and dark colors. I wanted to hide the part of my body I didn't like. But I was also hiding my hourglass waist, my cute hips, and my confidence. When I started dressing to highlight the parts of my body I loved, and became more neutral toward the parts I didn't like, it absolutely changed my game and boosted my self-assurance.

Dress respectfully.

Don't wear lingerie to a parent-teacher conference. Don't wear a tube top to an interview at a law office. Don't wear clothing that appropriates someone else's heritage or culture. Don't wear a bra that doesn't fit because you want to wear a certain cup size. Wear shoes with traction on icy days. You're smart, so use your good judgment!

Dress to feel good!

If wearing a crop top makes you happy, then wear it! But if it doesn't, that's okay; instead, rock the absolute hell out of your turtleneck. Wear what makes you feel good! Life's hard enough, you might as well wear the dang shorts.

Fashion adapts!

Before 2020, wearing face masks every day was almost unheard of in the US. But as of this writing, we are still wearing them, and they're likely to remain a part of our daily wardrobe for the foreseeable future. I have a mask in every single color to match every outfit. I have holiday ones, and fancy ones, and business-y ones, and cute disposable ones. Fashion will always adapt to the needs of society.

Embrace the ch-ch-ch-changes.

In my lifetime, I have already gone through several distinct fashion phases. In sixth grade, I was a hard-core church kid. I was really involved in my youth group and wore Christian band T-shirts and was annoying about it. By high school, I had become a hippie, and wore jeans splattered with paint and thrifted band shirts. Two years later, I evolved into a theatre kid. I wore black leggings and black shirts with big scarves and always looked like I was on my way to dance rehearsal. Now my style is hyper femme, colorful, and quirky cutie. Over all these transitions, I didn't "sell out" or "lose myself"—I just changed. Embrace the change. Remember and honor the past stages and move on up.

PUN FOR HIRE

JOB INTERVIEWS: They are SUPER intimidating, but at some point in life, most people will have to go on one. Whether it's for a part-time job while you're in school or for your dream career, an interview is bound to pop up.

As a person who has been on approximately 1,000 job interviews, I have some definite tips for not only how to look your best, but how to feel your best. I've had TONS of weird experiences on job interviews, meaning I've learned the hard lessons so you don't have to.

If you're anything like me, you've probably asked yourself a bunch of questions before an interview. Like, *What on earth do I WEAR to an interview? What do I say? What's the etiquette? Talking about myself makes me feel uncomfortable. WHAT IS BUSINESS CASUAL?!*

Honestly, after all this time, I'm still not entirely sure what "business casual" actually means, but I know that it's different from person to person and from industry to industry. It's one of those nebulous terms like "influencer" or "consultant" that basically means nothing concrete at all.

But real talk: How do you get the job? Well, much like a person who LOVES acrylics and polish, here's my advice for how to *nail* it!

Obviously, my tips and tricks are not hard-and-fast rules! Depending on the industry, the position, the geographical part of the country you live in, your age, etc., all this advice could be totally different. But this is a good place to start if you're feeling overwhelmed!

Style Tips

1. Dress comfortably.

This may feel counterintuitive, but if you're physically uncomfortable, it will read in your interview. Don't wear something that you're constantly going to be fidgeting in the whole time. Wear clothes that make you feel comfortable. Comfortable is when we feel our most confident!

2. Dress for the industry.

Wearing a full suit with six-inch heels and pearls for an interview with a start-up tech company or a quirky unicorn-print dress to work for a government office might send the wrong message. Check the company's website and social media to see if you can spot what other employees are wearing day to day. Or ask friends who work in similar industries.

3. If you would have gotten detention for it in middle school, don't wear it.

This includes a whole slew of things. Skirts should be longer than your fingertips, and necklines should be modest (as a busty gal, I realize this can be tricky!). Make sure there are no peeping bra straps or see-through blouses, and no dresses or skirts with thigh-high slits. No crop tops, no flip-flops, no ripped jeans. Keep your straps at least three fingers wide, etc. (Fun Fact: These are all REAL things that were part of my middle school dress code.) If your principal would have given you detention for wearing it, then it's probably not right for an interview.

4. Practice wearing your clothes.

This might seem so obvious, but when my mom passed this tip on to me, it BLEW MY MIND. Sit down in your outfit. Actually try it on and sit down. Make sure no buttons are popping, that no weird skin is exposed, that there's no gapping, and that it is equally comfortable to be sitting in as it is to stand in. Walk up and down some stairs (make sure you can do it in your shoes/skirt/dress combo). Wear it for an hour to make sure it doesn't wrinkle. Make sure it all fits and wears appropriately.

5. Give it some personality.

YOU have a personality. And expressing that effectively is half the interview. You're going to be spending a lot of time at your job. There is absolutely no sense in hiding your personality. For example, if you want to convey that you're fun and youthful, you might mix a subtle unicorn-print blouse with a pair of business trousers and a jacket. For many interviews, I have slipped in a novelty pattern or a bright color or polka dots with something a little more neutral. But if your personality is more of a blazer and pencil skirt in a neutral color, then let that shine! Just be true to you.

6. Keep everything else neutral.

Makeup should be natural-looking, not too heavy, and in natural tones. Keep that lime-green glitter eye shadow, purple mascara, and black lipstick for another day. Perfume should be incredibly subtle (two spritz max), or just don't wear it at all. Long, flashy fingernails are not usually the selling point at an interview. I usually would wash my hands with a fresh lemon to get that citrus smell. Pop a mint on your commute over. If the interviewer notices your makeup/smell/breath one way or the other, it's probably too strong.

7. Wear clothes that fit.

There's a lot of pressure on potential job candidates (especially plus-size ones, like myself) to wear something "corporate" or "professional." I am extremely busty, and since most button-down blouses gap, I have all but omitted them from my wardrobe. Buy clothes that fit your body size and shape. Get your pants hemmed if they're too long. It's when you wear what you're "supposed to" wear that you end up in clothes that are baggy or ill-fitting.

Interview Tips

1. Know what you bring to the table.

You might just need a job, but your interviewer needs someone who is going to add something to the position. What do you bring to the table? Lots of experience? Lots of education? A deep passion for the work? A special skill or certification? Are you super organized and efficient? Is your productivity through the roof? You might want to be on their team, but why should they want you on their team? If you can't answer that, it might not be the right fit.

2. Do your homework.

Research the company. See what big projects or goals they are currently working toward. Read what the company culture is like. Read the "About Us" tab on their website. Look at their LinkedIn page. Try to learn what the company values. All this information will come in handy during the interview. For example, I once interviewed at a college, and mentioned their football team casually. Everyone else in the room chuckled, before telling me they don't have a football team. I'm pretty sure I lost the interview in that moment.

3. Don't lie, but keep your honesty in check.

You need to be able to actually do the job you're interviewing for. You should have all the skills listed in the job posting. However, there are ways to sell yourself in areas that you lack. For example, if someone asks you how you are with Excel, but it's been a few years since you had to use it, an appropriate answer would be, "I'm good with Excel, but I could always use a quick refresher on any updates." Frame everything— even your faults—in a professional way. Never lie about what you can or cannot do, but if they ask about a skill you don't have but think you can learn, an appropriate answer is, "I'm not familiar with that, but I'm always happy to learn a new skill. I'm a quick study."

4. Don't bad-mouth anyone.

It's so easy to want to complain about your former/current position when an interviewer asks why you're looking for a new job. But talking trash on your boss or the company makes YOU look bad. It's best to be honest, but professional. Instead of saying that you HATED your old boss because he was a big jerkface, a better answer would be that management changed and you felt like you no longer fit as well with the company culture. You got fired? Say that you're looking for a new challenge to expand your skills. You didn't get paid enough? Say that you love your job but it isn't sustainable long-term. This may seem silly, but framing your answers in a positive light will show that you're a positive person.

No matter what, make sure that you and your skills are what stand out the most! Your outfit should be so flawless that your interviewers barely even have to think about it in comparison to your badass self.

5. Be polite.

This is so simple, but you'd be amazed how many people forget it. Greet, smile at, and be polite to the receptionist. Shake the interviewer's hand when they come out to meet you. Smile. Thank them for meeting with you as you walk out the door. Making a personal connection can go a long way. Know the name of every person you're going to be interviewing with. Call them by their name. Cover your mouth if you sneeze. Say thank you. Manners aren't just for kindergartners!

6. It's okay to take a second.

If you're asked a question that you don't have an answer to, it's okay to take a beat and come up with a good answer. I usually just say, "Ooh, that's a great question, give me a moment to come up with a great answer." Take a beat, take a breath, think, and answer carefully. It's so tempting to say the first thing that comes to mind, but it's okay to ask for a moment. It'll only buy you a second or two, but that can make all the difference between sounding like you're scrambling and sounding like you're thoughtful.

7. Be confident!

Tell the interviewer (professionally) how awesome you are! This is a time to talk about yourself. Don't be shy about your skills and accomplishments. It can feel weird to boast about yourself, but literally, that's what this is. It's thirty minutes of professional bragging. Own it.

THE PRESTON TEST

I SWEAR TO TELL THE WHOLE TRUTH, most of the truth (to keep it PG), so help me blog.

My husband, Preston, and I met on a dating app in June 2014. Sometimes we just tell people we met at our local community theatre, EPAC, because the only reason I even messaged him back was that in his very first message, he asked if I knew EPAC. I was always so nervous about getting murdered from online dating that I basically never messaged anyone back. I had never met ANYONE from the internet, let alone gone on a date with one of these potential cold-blooded killers. (Side note: This paragraph made me realize I've listened to one too many episodes of *My Favorite Murder.*)

However, this boy mentioned EPAC, where I happened to have started working full-time about two weeks earlier. His first message said, "Hey, I see you're really into theatre, have you ever heard of EPAC?" Bam. I messaged back and said, "Funnily enough, I'm in EPAC . . . right this moment."

We ended up hitting it off. So, I did what any girl does, and I asked EVERY-ONE at the theatre about him. Was he nice? Was he cute? Was he talented? Was he gross? What's his deal? Everyone confirmed that he was nice . . . but weird. "Nice" and "weird" are two of my favorite words, so this was only getting better. Around that same time, my boss posted a video on the theatre's Facebook page . . . with Preston singing. Folks, my husband has PIPES. He is an incredible actor and singer. When I saw that video of him singing, my theatre-kid heart grew three sizes and I decided I had to go on a date with him.

A few weeks went by while we chatted through the app. I suggested we become Facebook friends and gave him my phone number. And here's where the story almost gets tragic.

HE DIDN'T CALL. Or text. Or do anything. He just sat around having my phone number. I sent him another message or two on Facebook in the following days while he was sitting around and not texting me or calling me . . . or asking me on a date. Our communication fizzled.

Almost a month later, I was camping with some friends, when I got a text from a random number that said, "Hey, it's Preston. Blah blah blah."

I made a face, put my phone away, and thought, *Yeah, right, buddy. I give you my number and you don't call for nearly a month. No way.* I never answered him, but I never deleted his number. I did what Preston now calls "ghosting him." I took his shyness and awkwardness with the ladies as a personal snub, so I stopped responding.

Two more months went by. I dated other people. Kissed other people. Just had good twentysomething fun. I had regrets about breaking up with my last boyfriend (who sucked). I moved in with my friend Joe. Preston and I didn't speak or try to get in contact again.

That fall, Preston was in a production of *Cabaret* at EPAC. One night, I was working late in the theatre's upstairs offices and he was rehearsing downstairs. Since I made the schedules, I knew he was there, and despite the past few months, I wanted to meet him. I figured, *What's the harm?* I decided I would wait until rehearsal was over to leave and hope to bump into him.

An hour went by. Two hours. Three hours. I got tired of waiting, so I left. When I got home, I sent him a text that said I was sad we didn't meet. He texted me back right away. Our natural chemistry and banter picked up again. Like we'd never missed a beat.

At the time, I was also in a theatre production (*Carrie: The Musical*—yeah, like pig's-blood-at-the-prom *Carrie*), and we both had crazy different schedules. There was essentially no time to meet in person. We continued to text, but still weren't able to meet face-to-face.

Because we were in the same building every day, we started writing little sticky-note messages to each other. I would hide them in his costume pockets with little snacks or treats. He would leave notes and my favorite drink on my desk. We wrote miniature love letters to each other every night on 3×3 squares. My heart would skip a beat each time I found another one. I still have every single sticky note he left for me.

Our shows opened on the same night and we told each other to break a leg. Due to timing things, my show's run closed a few nights before his did, so I decided to go one night.

That day, I'm restless at work. Pacing. Munching on my pearls. Reapplying my lipstick. I get hardly any work done. I was a really annoying coworker.

Finally, it's time for the show to start, so I go up and sit in the audience. I made my best friend Joe (who is one of the best-looking dudes I know) come with me. You know, in case of murderers. The show begins, and there he is onstage. I'm clutching Joe's arm to calm myself down. My leg is jiggling. There he is, thirty feet in front of me, and we can't say hello yet.

The show ends and I'm ticking down the moments until he gets out of the dressing room and comes upstairs.

Then I have this big realization: Joe has to leave. The man has literally done modeling and is, like, the guy in our group of friends who everyone has had a crush on at one point. He's SO handsome. I can't bring this tall, gorgeous dude on my first date. Like, who does that? TG Joe, being the best friend ever, doesn't mind that I was quickly shooing him out the door. (Don't worry, Joe was my man of honor at my and Preston's wedding on that same stage!)

I wait upstairs for Preston. Eventually he comes up and we meet. Right there in the middle of the stage, on top of the trapdoor. He gives me a big hug. It's a little awkward. He tells me he thought I'd be taller. I tell him I felt the same way. We laugh a little awkwardly.

We chat for a few minutes and decide he'll grab his stuff and we'll go to a local bar to get to know each other better and have a few drinks.

A few hours later, and the bar is starting to close. We aren't done talking. So we go to this gorgeous and quiet park and walk around under the streetlamps with the mist and the fog and talk more. We kiss for the first time that night.

Our story started when two theatre kids fell in love.

WE'VE BEEN DATING EVER SINCE.

After two dates, I remember going home to Joe and saying, "Yeah, I'm going to marry that guy. I just know it. It's a weird gut feeling." Soon after, we started using the B- and G-words, officially.

Three years later, he would get down on one knee on the same stage at the same community theatre and ask me to marry him. And a year after that, we would get married on that same stage.

For years before this, I was terrified of dating. Dating seemed complicated and scary. When I was fourteen years old, the first boy I ever kissed told me I was too fat for him to date in public at school. I was devastated, and basically became a relationship-phobe after that. I did not want a boyfriend at all—I just didn't want to get myself into that. I had boys ask me out over the years, and I turned them down. I was all about kissing boys on the down-low, in someone else's parents' finished basements. I craved boys who kept me secret.

When I did date, I sometimes met extremely nice but extremely dull men and women who didn't seem likely to break my heart, but who definitely would be able to bore me to tears. Dating seemed like a thing that wasn't meant for me. It wasn't meant for fat girls.

When I met Preston, my opinion on dating changed completely. He just meshed so perfectly with me. I felt loved, safe, desired, sexy, smart, valued, and honored. I didn't know I could feel that way with a partner. I had always assumed I would end up with a partner who "tolerated" or "fetishized" my body instead of embracing it, because until I met Preston, I wasn't sure a person like him existed.

When I was still actively dating, I didn't struggle with what to wear. I struggled with having to put my fat body in a vulnerable place to be judged by a stranger. It gave me so much anxiety about dating that I basically dreaded the idea of dating at all. I loved the idea of having a partner, but the thought of being fat on a date put me off the idea forever.

I could give you fashion tips until the cows come home, but the short answer is, for a date, dress like yourself and dress appropriately for your activity. What you'd wear for a rock-climbing date would be totally different from your outfit for a date to a comic convention. Wear something that makes you feel confident. Dress like you plan on turning heads. Dress with some level of comfort, or else you'll look uncomfortable. Let your playful and sexy sides peek out a bit, with a smidge of slut. (We support sluts here!) Obviously, your looks for a picnic date and a date to the opera would be totally different, so keep in mind that you need to FEEL like a million bucks no matter where the date takes you!

Instead of fashion tips, let me introduce you to my totally custom "Preston Test," which you can use when sizing up any potential partner.

The Preston Test*

(*This quiz works for any committed partners!)

1. If you ask them what their type is and they don't have one, that's a HUGE green flag! We love a partner who sees people, not body types.

2. Are they the same brand of weird as you? For Preston and me, our brand of weird is "adult theatre kids." We love to listen to the musical *Ragtime* (1998 OBC) in our car in the parking lot at two in the morning so we can belt without waking up the neighbors.

3. Are they careful with your vulnerability? Before we met, I messaged Preston and said, "You know I'm plus-size, right?" because I was paranoid that I'd be accused of catfishing for using a good picture that made me look too thin. Preston answered that he knew and that he didn't care, he was just excited to see me.

4. Do they respect your boundaries when you set them? This is critical for anyone going on a date. If they try to overstep a boundary that you intentionally set, throw a red flag on the field immediately.

5. Are your fights about whatever you're actually fighting about? Is a fight about the dishes turning into an argument about how you feel like you can't trust them? Those arguments are when it's time to wave a red flag and march on.

6. If they are constantly talking about how much they like your body, referring to you as a BBW over and over again, asking you to eat in front of them, mentioning gaining weight, only taking you on food-related dates, or saying that they exclusively date fat people—well, that's a fetish flag for sure. If you like the fetishization, then no judgment, but be sure you know the difference and you know what you're getting into.

7. Would almost any activity be better with them? For real, everything is more fun with Preston by my side. The airport is better with him. Grocery shopping is better with him. Holidays, seeing a movie, traveling, good days, bad days, all the days—they're all better with him.

8. Are your dates public? There's sometimes a stigma that you should hide your date if they're fat. Sometimes people will only take you on dates to dark theatres or clubs, will insist on hanging out at home, or won't introduce you to friends. Date someone who is proud to show you off to people, not someone who treats you like a guilty pleasure.

9. Is there best friend potential? Preston is my best friend. There's no one in the whole world I'd rather spend my time with.

10. If your first date was food-related, did you feel comfortable enough to order what you actually wanted to eat? I went on dates where I ordered salad or something very light and lean because I was too nervous to eat a big burger in front of the person sitting across from me.

11. Do they make time for you? Don't waste your dating energy on people who can't spend their time on you.

(**Author's Note:** Don't trust anyone who says they're "a nice guy" or "drama-free" in their dating profile. That's the biggest red flag there is that they are probably not very nice or that they are all drama.)

Not Your Mother's Dating Game

When I was a teenager, my mom told me I shouldn't expect to get married until I was in my thirties or forties, when people stopped caring about fat bodies so much because expectations were lower once people got a little older and the dating pool got smaller. Well, she couldn't have been more wrong. I met Preston when I was twenty-two and we were married when I was twenty-six.

First of all, there's absolutely nothing wrong with getting married in your thirties or forties or not choosing marriage at all. Second, the world is changing. The narrative on fat bodies is changing. Don't fear the dating world your mother or grandmother or big sister grew up in.

I had my first kiss at fourteen in my parents' finished basement. (We've all kissed a person in someone's parents' finished basements, amirite?) When the boy went home that night, he called me (on the landline, lol) and told me I was just too big for him to date at school, so I couldn't tell anyone that we had kissed. At first, I was so sad. I thought that if we kissed, we were gearing up to go steady or whatever we were calling it back in 2006. But I felt like that was what I deserved, as a fat girl. I was fat and ugly and deserved to be kept hidden. I had a long streak of kissing boys with girlfriends because it felt like there was "no other option" than keeping it a secret. It made me believe I had no choice in the matter.

When I was in college, I had a crush on my best friend. He knew it. We kissed once at a party in a scuzzy university kitchen, and it was like kissing a cousin. No chemistry at all. My crush fizzled and turned into a great friendship. A few years later, I asked him why he didn't like me back then. And he reluctantly admitted that it was my body.

Another boy I pined after for years and years eventually pretty much told me that the reason he wasn't with me was because of my weight. He was sexually attracted to me, but he didn't like my fat body. He was embarrassed by it. It was a thing he had to get past. It finally escalated to us having sex, and afterward, he said, "I wanted to see if having sex would change how I feel about you." Spoiler alert: It did not change how he felt about me, or my body.

It was so demoralizing that men treated me this way, but I have to ask myself: Why, at any point in time, did I even want to date people who didn't value my body or who treated me like I was something to be ashamed of? I actively and openly wanted to date all these men, but they all out-and-out told me they didn't like my body or wanted to hide our relationship. Weirdly, at some point, this became the easiest rejection to swallow. After all, attraction is attraction, and I shouldn't want to date someone who isn't attracted to me. Period. You should have zero desire to be in a romantic or sexual relationship with someone who sees your literal body as a roadblock or hurdle to overcome.

If you take absolutely nothing else away from this chapter, please take this thought at least: Don't stop dating. The first time I kissed a boy, I was told I was too fat. What if I had just stopped or given up or refused to take up space because of a few bad dates?

Spoiler alert: They're all bad dates until you meet the right one.

LET'S TALK ABOUT SEX, BABY

I LIKE SEX.

If that is a radical idea to you . . . well, should it be? If you're actively having sex and it's a consensual act between two adults, you should like it. In fact, you should really like it. I might even go so far as to say that I think you should love it. It's okay if you don't like it, but if that is the case, you shouldn't be doing it. If you're participating, it's meant to be a fun activity.

Okay, I know that since we're talking about sex, some of you are already uncomfortable. That's okay. Let's sit with that discomfort for a minute and we can come back and revisit it later. If we're still not ready later, that's okay—this chapter will be here for you whenever you're ready. No rush.

1. Every body jiggles.

Literally every single person. We are all out here jiggling. Our thighs, our tummies, our upper-arm fat, our butts, our back rolls—we are all out here jiggling together. You have to remember that jiggling is a universal experience, no matter what body size you are.

2. Do you think your partner is stupid?

Nobody took you home from the bar and magically thought you were going to be a size 2 under your clothes. Taking an educated guess between what a person looks like clothed and what a person looks like naked is honestly not that hard. Why would you think that you suddenly need to be a rail-thin model the second you take your pants off? They saw you dressed. The person you brought home to bang isn't dumb; they know how human bodies work.

3. No one is thinking about you as much as you're thinking about you.

Making sure that your room is clean and your sheets smell nice is typically the easiest way to make sure that you aren't going to offend anyone in the boudoir. Don't worry too much about glitter body lotion and perfectly shaved legs. Enjoy the moment.

4. Communicate your discomfort.

If you're in a position that simply doesn't work, then tell your partner and switch it up. It's not the end of the world. Sometimes positions don't work no matter what your body size is. It's totally normal. Let your partner know it's not working. They may not even know that it hurts or is pinching you weird. You have to communicate. Literally no one wants to be out here in a bad banging position.

5. Stop apologizing for your body.

Instead of saying sorry for your love handles or back fat, try saying nothing. You don't need to excuse your body, or mention that it's being worked on, or apologize for its shape. Catch yourself every time you're about to say sorry.

6. Ain't no shame in the kink game.

As long as everyone is on board with whatever you're doing, embrace it. Mix in some handcuffs, or some warm wax, or a blindfold. Embrace your desire to wear a costume. Let's get kinky!

7. They are probably pumped to bang.

Your partner probably didn't get all the way to nudity only to suddenly see your naked body and change their mind because of that. People change their mind for all kinds of reasons, so communicating and respecting boundaries are important, but the reasons behind that change of feeling are seldomly based on body image.

8. Masturbate more.

It's totally natural. Get in tune with your body and your sexuality. Knowing what you like and being able to connect with yourself better are going to bring nothing but positive results for your sex life.

9. Pillows & lube.

Pillows are great for getting into positions and helping the flow of movement a little bit (especially for fat-bottomed babes like me). And lube is your friend. It's not a reflection of poor performance on either party's part. It's only going to make it a better time. That's a tip from me to you.

10. Own the bedroom.

Your confidence is always going to be the sexiest thing in the bedroom. No matter how hot your lingerie or how dirty your talking, you being excited about your body will continue to be a showstopper. Think of how Lizzo totally owns her body; she is a total sex icon.

11. Lingerie comes in every size.

If you're having a tough time feeling sexy, splurge and treat yourself to a sexy bra or a revealing teddy. Lingerie is designed to amp up the sensual vibes. I've seen lingerie in up to a 6X or 7X, so don't tell me they don't make it in your size.

12. Sex is supposed to be fun.

Let it be fun. Remove some of your own stigma and enjoy it! Your body is not a limitation. Your body, at any size, should not hinder your ability to have pleasurable and consensual sex. You can make any position work, you can utilize toys and lube, you can wear lingerie. Your actual body is preventing you from doing very little; it's your body image that's really keeping you from going for it.

13. Sex is naturally goofy.

Sex is goofy. Sometimes a queef sneaks out or you fart when moving positions. Sometimes a position is a total fail. I once was with a guy who moaned like a dying cat and I laughed out loud. Preston fell off the side of the bed once. In college, after reuniting with my boyfriend, a bunch of my friends broke into my apartment WHILE WE WERE IN BED TOGETHER to steal my DVD of our student play. So allow yourself to laugh when it's funny.

For most people, sex and dating are part of life. You basically can't avoid being nude forever. It's next to impossible. If you and your partner can make it less intimidating and more intimate, then that is a success.

I remember that, for so long, I hid under covers or with the lights off before being able to truly embrace my sexuality. I cried after most encounters because I felt like my partner was merely tolerating my body and not appreciating or celebrating it with me. I wanted to feel desired. It took years to feel like I could just enjoy sex.

So my advice for you, my goddess, is to embrace your inner Aphrodite now. You'll be thankful you did.

HOLY MATRIMONY, BATMAN!

WE'VE ALL GOTTEN ONE (OR THE FIRST OF, LIKE, SEVEN) "SAVE THE DATE" CARDS. I am willing to bet that at least once in your life, you have been called to buy your friend, neighbor, or cousin a bread maker or a rice cooker, RSVP'ed, and shared in their big day! Maybe you're married? Planning a wedding? Part of a bridal party for the first time? Then you know there's A LOT to consider. Weddings can range from super simple to super intricate and expensive, small to big, and include a variety of cultural traditions, exotic destinations, and unusual requests. But why am I describing weddings to you?

Because no matter what side of the aisle you're on—be it as a bride, bridesmaid, staff, or guest—weddings are STRESSFUL. For everyone. Or they can be.

I remember feeling so stressed on my own wedding day that when it was all over, I just cried from relief. Now, I loved my wedding and was the LEAST bridezilla bride ever . . . but that night, I just cried for a solid ten minutes—it felt like such a relief that I could stop worrying about things.

Half the problem of weddings is figuring out what to wear. You can't wear white as a guest. Are the bridesmaids wearing matching jewelry? How do you incorporate something blue?! Can you dance in the shoes you want? Is the groom's strict Catholic family going to judge your plunging sequined neckline as you take Communion? Is your outfit going to hold up for eight hours? While being photographed a TON? Plus, you have to sit, stand, walk, dance, eat, drink, and drive in the outfit. That is a LONG checklist for ONE outfit. Yes, friends, there are a lot of considerations going into weddings.

And obviously, the further up the aisle you are, the more stressful it is.

So let's break it down (*a little bit softer now*), grab some Jordan almonds, register for all this advice, and talk about some wedding fashion.

Wedding Guest

One of the first weddings I attended was that of a family friend I had known since childhood. I was SO pumped!

Now, the dress code was listed as "semiformal." Which might be the most subjective style designation ever. My mom and I argued about what it meant: She said it meant you could only wear dark colors or gem tones as a guest. I said it had more to do with the cut and the fabric. The internet weighed in and said it's about length, necklines, cost of dress, etc. It was tough to find out exactly what that meant. The general consensus: WHO KNOWS?! We went with our gut and it turned out fine.

But there're plenty more dress-code styles you might encounter out there. So let's sort out all the different "attires" you might see listed on your invite!

BLACK TIE: An evening gown or a very chic cocktail dress! Satin, lace, silk, etc. Darker or jewel-tone colors. Jewelry is definitely appropriate!

For men: A cummerbund and a black bow tie with a tuxedo.

FORMAL: A cocktail dress or a tea-length dress or a fitted suit. Again, heavier, more intricate fabric like satin or something crepe.

For men: A tuxedo or a dark suit.

COCKTAIL ATTIRE: A cocktail dress, a jumpsuit, a shorter dress. This is a time for brighter colors, patterns, fun accessories, etc.

For men: A seasonal suit.

SEMIFORMAL: A cute day dress, a fun patterned dress, a skirt and blouse.

For men: A suit and tie or slacks with no jacket, a button-down and a tie.

CASUAL: A casual dress, pants and a nice blouse, a romper with a sweater.

For men: No tie, no coat, but a nice button-down and slacks are always a good choice! "Casual" does not mean shorts and flip-flops, unless you're on a tropical island.

Some Definite Dos & Don'ts of Wedding Guest Attire

Do:

WEAR SOMETHING MODERATELY COMFORTABLE. There will probably be dancing.

BRING A PAIR OF FLIP-FLOPS IN THE CAR (in case of blisters from dancing).

BRING A CLUTCH. All you should need at a wedding are lipstick and mascara, a tampon/pad, a hair elastic, some cash, and an ID for the bar. Everything else is a luxury!

LAYER IF YOU CAN! If you're moving between inside and outside at any point, then the temperature will vary. Plan ahead.

BE CONSIDERATE OF THE BRIDE AND GROOM WHEN PLANNING YOUR OUTFIT. Theoretically, you know them. At my wedding, I had a friend wear red sequined pants and a red sequined blazer with no shirt underneath and some sexy stilettos. I LOVED IT! He looked AMAZING! But we are vibrant, colorful, theatrical people, and we encouraged lots of personality. Some couples and families might be more conservative or reserved, or have cultural or religious differences. Dress accordingly.

Don't:

DON'T WEAR WHITE. It's a totally weird party move. Even if it's a cultural tradition for not-the-bride to wear white, leave your white summer dress at home!

DON'T WEAR HIGH HEELS if part of the wedding takes place on grass. You'll get stuck.

DON'T WEAR WRINKLED CLOTHES. Steam them. Iron them. If you have neither a steamer nor an iron, put the item in your bathroom and run the shower on the hottest setting with the door closed for ten minutes.

DON'T TRY TO OUTSHINE ANYONE! This isn't your day!

DON'T FEEL PRESSURED TO DROP BIG MONEY ON SOMETHING TO WEAR. You can find cute weddingwear at the thrift store or at discount stores like Ross, T.J.Maxx, and Target, or by repurposing pieces you already have!

DON'T WEAR SOMETHING THAT SHOWS SWEAT MARKS EASILY. You'll likely be sweating, no matter what time of year it is. It's better not to have huge pit marks.

Bridesmaid

My friend Rachel was one of my first "peers" to get married. I'd been to the weddings of older friends and family before, but Rachel was the first person in my age group to get hitched, which felt AMAZING, and totally weird, if I'm being honest.

It was also my first time being in a wedding party.

And unfortunately, watching Kristen Wiig in *Bridesmaids* did NOT prepare me enough for the journey I was about to go on.

As you know, I lovelovelove having my picture taken (because I am so damn photogenic), and weddings are the perfect excuse to have my picture taken with my hair and makeup done perfectly. So I was so down for being a bridesmaid.

Now, the bride, her maid of honor (MOH), her (now) husband, and their families were so kind, generous, welcoming, helpful, and amazing, so ALL the stumbles and little hurdles I encountered that day are completely on me for not knowing what the heck I was doing. That being said, I had so much fun and made so many great memories. I was so lucky to stand by my friend's side as she said "I do."

1. It is expensive.

Budget. Budget. Budget. Budget. Make sure you can afford to be part of the wedding party if you say you can. I was very fortunate to have a wonderful friend and bride who helped out financially where she could.

Don't ever go into being a bridesmaid (or particularly a maid of honor) without expecting to spend money. Between the dress, alterations, shoes, travel, tolls, hotel rooms, food for travel, accessories (tights, shapewear, etc.), and gifts for the bridal shower, bachelorette party, and wedding—it can add up. You can expect to spend up to $1,000 to be in even a very moderate wedding, with the average cost being at least $1,600, per The Knot.

2. Plan to be plus.

At this wedding, both the bride and her MOH were very petite women. I was the only plus-size member of the bridal party, and I definitely felt that way throughout the course of the day.

Make sure you have jewelry extenders if you are all wearing matching jewelry. I had to wear a necklace that wouldn't close around my neck, so I MacGyvered an extension out of a safety pin, broken metal, and a prayer that my hair would cover how ugly it looked in the back!

Let your friend know what size you wear so when she starts looking for matching dresses, she'll know what sizes need to be available. If you need extra-wide shoes, a dress that accommodates a bra, or anything else, let her know!

Make sure you bring your own pantyhose/spare bra/shapewear/etc. It's really hard to grab a spare pair at the last minute, and there are seldom extra plus-size pairs floating around.

Make sure you are mentally prepared to be "the fat one." Now, to be sure, no one there made me feel that way at Rachel's wedding. I had a wonderful time with the other 'maids! But it's hard not to feel that way, and it can definitely make you feel like an outlier when you can't close the petite bracelets or there's a safety pin holding your necklace together or you have to wear a bra and it pokes out the back of your dress.

Communicate clearly and respectfully with your friend early on to be considerate of those things! If it isn't part of their personal experience, they aren't trying to exclude you; they honestly have probably never thought about having G-cup boobs that can't free-boob and haven't met a strapless up to the task yet.

3. *You'll definitely start thinking about your own wedding.*

Preston and I definitely stood there and started talking about our flowers, our food, our pictures, venue, ceremony, etc. Whatever it was that we were looking at, we started discussing all the things we would want for our own wedding.

We weren't even engaged at the time, and we felt inspired! We took note of things we did like (a brief ceremony) and things we didn't like (a formal sit-down dinner) and started using them as guideposts for our own wedding.

4. *Drink in moderation.*

At a lot of weddings, there are always guests who overdo it on the drinks. Like, seventeen sheets to the wind. Now, I'm not saying that you need to be Sober Sally. But it's just not classy to be that bridesmaid or groomsman who is SLOPPY by five p.m.

At Rachel's wedding, we had a bottle of wine in the bridal suite; everyone sipped wine casually throughout the day and it was fine, because that is moderation.

If you consume alcohol (and you don't have to!), then drink safely, and for funsies! Pace yourself, plan to not have to drive home, and drink lots of water.

Because, friends, it's a good rule of thumb in life that you SHOULD ALWAYS STRIVE TO NOT BE *THAT* GUY.

5. You'll do it.

Theoretically, the person you have elected to stand beside as they create a lasting union with a life partner is someone you like and care for very much.

If they ask you to do something, just do it.

And I mean WHATEVER it is. Just do it.

If it's holding their dress up so they can pee, if it's holding their boobs up so you can nipple tape them, if it's constantly moving their train so it will ALWAYS photograph well, dealing with a drunk relative, running back to get the thing they forgot, supergluing a penny to your shoe, etc., well, just do it. It is their day, and it's awesome to have the honor to stand by their side. This day is the ultimate in friendship goals. Don't make it about you!

6. Schedules are key.

Both Rachel and her MOH were super type A. They had spreadsheets of when everyone needed to be everywhere. And I mean *everyone*: the bride's parents, the kids, the groom's parents, each individual bridesmaid and groomsman. It was AMAZING.

It was just so organized that I did not feel like we had a lot of stress. We weren't late or behind. The intense organization made the day feel seamless.

You always need at least one or two type A personalities in a bridal party, or else nothing is going to happen. And Rachel's MOH was amazing. All the charts. All the organization. I highly recommend it.

7. In the famous words of Simba's crazy uncle Scar, be prepared.

The day of Rachel's wedding, the bridal party needed a lot of things I hadn't even realized we would need: makeup setter, safety pins, deodorant, superglue, Tums and ibuprofen, pads and tampons, hairspray, and hair ties, to name a few.

Luckily, the MOH had us COVERED. She had a bag that would put Mary Poppins's to shame, full of every supply we could possibly need. And we needed most everything in it at least once. Make sure you have that day-of, just-in-case wedding bag.

8. Shape up.

Wear shapewear. Normally I'm super opposed to it. But you will be photographed from EVERY angle. And not every angle is flattering. And there's so much food and drink that you're likely to bloat a little bit. It just makes a happier time for all.

I wore shapewear for Rachel's wedding, and honestly, I was SO happy with that decision.

9. Getting ready is half the fun.

Make sure there's good tunes, coffee, and comfy clothes. For Rachel's wedding, we all came wearing comfy outfits (including shirts we could take off without messing up our hair) and completely sans makeup.

Also, make sure you have some ideas for hair/makeup for the gals who are helping you! (And tipping never hurts, either!)

10. Doing stuff in a bridesmaid dress is hard.

This one is pretty self-explanatory. Peeing was so freaking strenuous. As was walking on grass, sitting, dancing, etc. It's basically unavoidable, so be ready for it.

11. It's really a great experience.

It's wonderful to get to stand by a best friend, to tear up with joy and with pride, to dance, laugh, cry, and look gorgeous! And it's also a great experience to have your hair and makeup done. It's awesome to get to look so beautiful for a day.

But mostly, it's such a happy, loving, and important moment that you can't picture being anywhere else other than right at the bride's side.

FUNNY STORY INTERRUPTION

SO, THERE IS APPARENTLY THIS WEIRD TRADITION (that I had never even heard of until Rachel's wedding) where you glue a penny to your shoe? And it's supposed to be for luck or something?

(Pause, while I ask Preston. He's made it to the audition round of *Jeopardy!* on three different occasions. He always knows this stuff.)

According to Preston, it comes from the saying "Something old, something new, something borrowed, something blue," which used to end with "and a sixpence in your shoe." Evidently, the sixpence was meant to symbolize wealth for the newlyweds (Americans now just use pennies).

Okay.

So, in the limo on our way to the photo location, Rachel (the bride) remembers this tradition and is sad she didn't do it. But the MOH whips out some superglue and a 2016 penny and we decide to superglue it to the bottom of Rachel's shoe.

I decide that this is my "I'll do it" moment and volunteer to do the gluing. Despite my long history of being clumsy and having bad hand-eye coordination, I decide to make this my moment to SHINE!

A red light comes—we are in FULL gowns, hair, and makeup—and I quickly open the superglue, spread it on the penny . . . and JUST then, the limo starts to move and the penny starts to slide off the shoe (because I hadn't flipped it over yet). To prevent it from falling, I snatch it out of midair.

I quick flip it back onto the shoe and glue it down.

Then I realize MY FINGERS ARE SUPERGLUED TOGETHER.

Like, my index, middle, and thumb all got superglued together. I try to pull them apart but it is ripping my skin. Now I'm having to face the reality that I might have to take ALL of these photos with my fingers glued together, doing a one-handed chicken dance, not even being able to pick up my bouquet! Your girl was mortified.

Luckily, the MOH, who is also a medical professional, whipped out nail polish remover to soak through the glue.

All of this while we're in a moving limo.

After a few minutes, thanks to the MOH's quick thinking, the glue loosened, but I seriously was laughing so hard that I was crying. It was so ridiculous, but it all worked out!

Your Own Wedding

My own wedding was awesome. And stressful. And fun. I was fortunate enough that my mom planned a lot of it. To her credit, she planned our wedding. It was so "us"—my mom really has a knack for events!

I wanted our wedding to have the aesthetic of the movie *Up*, meaning lots of kitsch and quirkiness, with a good dash of rainbow! And with a ton of help from my mom and a small village, I totally think our dream came to life.

My wedding to Preston was a mix of eclectic, small-town charm, retro, and color. Our centerpieces were thrifted vases with floral arrangements and vintage board games. Preston and I got to sneak away to take pictures at our local town fair. We had monkey bread cupcakes and a food truck, and our first dance was to a show tune.

We had fun details around every corner, from the thrifted or flea market tablecloths to vases from the 1950s to maple syrup as our wedding favor. There were balloons and big velvet couches with rainbow lanterns. We got married in the theatre where we met (seriously perfect), and we painted the stage pink.

After the reception, we ended the night by hitting our favorite theatre bar and keeping the party going! The night was filled to the brim with small-town charm.

Check out this wedding picture:

We transformed the stage into an absolute dream.

(Photography credit to David Gerz, who took our wedding pics! I had very high expectations for this photography, and he did NOT fail to deliver.)

Tips for Brides

For your bridesmaids:

1. COMMUNICATE CLEARLY WHAT YOUR EXPECTATIONS ARE AS EARLY AS YOU CAN. What kind of dress, shoes, accessories, hair, activities, budget, travel, and time commitment are you expecting? It's your job to make sure everyone is on the same page, and is able to meet your financial and time expectations.

2. ALL BODIES ARE CREATED DIFFERENT. Halters don't look good on everyone. Backless or strapless is nearly impossible for some. Body shapes, heights, and comfort levels are all different! I usually suggest not picking the exact same dress for your squad (even though I did). Pick a color scheme, a theme, a few key words, or whatever and let your bridal party find their own looks! It's so much easier and simpler (for you and them), and it will ultimately look better to have a group of people in outfits that actually fit their bodies as opposed to something uniform.

3. ASIDE FROM DECIDING ON A DRESS, MAKE SURE YOU COMMUNICATE YOUR WISHES for hair, makeup, shoes, etc.

4. BE MINDFUL OF BUDGETS. Not everyone can afford a massive budget, which is also why letting people pick out their own attire is easier. My bridesmaids' dresses were under $100, and I let them decide on their own shoes.

5. BE KIND TO YOUR BRIDAL PARTY! They are there to help, and setting clear expectations is one way to minimize stress later on down the road.

6. PLAN TO HAVE YOUR BRIDESMAID OUTFITS READY— everything delivered, altered, pressed, and ready to go—at least a month out from the wedding. Which means other decisions should be made a few months beforehand.

For your guests:

1. MAKE SURE YOU NOTE ANY ATTIRE SPECIFICS on your invitation, your wedding website, and anywhere else! People mostly are lazy and will forget, so make the info readily available.

2. BE REASONABLE. Asking every VIBRANT and kooky theatre person at our wedding to dress modestly would have gone over like a lead balloon. On the same note, if most of your friends are artists, freelancers, or work in the service industry, then having a black-tie wedding might financially prevent some guests from being able to be there on your big day.

3. SHARE THE TRADITION OR SIGNIFICANCE OF SPECIFIC ATTIRE REQUESTS. I attended the wedding of a friend who is Hawaiian, and there were lots of leis for guests to wear and she shared their significance! It can be a great way to share culture with friends.

4. IF THERE IS A CULTURAL NEED FOR GUESTS TO DRESS A CERTAIN WAY, THEN MAKE SURE YOUR GUESTS KNOW THAT IS THE EXPECTATION. Particularly if you have a conservative or religious family!

5. DON'T GET ANNOYED WHEN PEOPLE ASK YOU WHAT TO WEAR! Actually tell them what you want. They're asking because they want to do the right thing.

6. THINK ABOUT YOUR OVERALL AESTHETIC AND BASE YOUR WEDDING DRESS CODE ON THAT. My attire was listed as "Semiformal, the more color the better!" and our friends and family did not disappoint!

For yourself:

1. PICKING A WEDDING DRESS IS DAUNTING, BUT LUCKILY, THE INTERNET IS ROBUST. Figuring out a few key words for style will go a long way!

Here's a brief list of style things you should be considering and some of the options that you might see:

- **Length:** long, ankle-length, tea-length, short
- **Cut:** A-line, trumpet, mermaid, ball gown, column
- **Color:** pure white, off-white, blush
- **Details:** lace, satin, pearl, flowers, crystals
- **Time of Year:** winter wedding, summer wedding
- **Theme/Vibe:** beach wedding, *Downton Abbey*

2. COMFORT MATTERS! When you're picking out your dress, you'll have to be in it for approximately eight to twelve hours, have your picture taken approximately a zillion times, and have to look at those pictures for the next thirty years. Comfort matters! I knew I needed to wear a bra and that I didn't want to wear a slimming garment, so I picked a dress that fit both those requirements. If you're full-busted (like me) and will constantly be tugging up a strapless dress, well, you'll be worried about that all night. If you're short and clumsy (also like me), a floor-length gown might make you nervous about tripping. What makes you feel your best? Find THAT dress.

3. YOU DON'T NEED TO CHANGE YOURSELF. If you think you NEED to lose weight, change your hair, wear a shaping garment, or change your physical appearance to fit a specific dress, then that is not the dress for you.

How I Found My Dress

Let's rewind back to 2015, when I started Pinterest-ing things for my wedding. I typed in the magical phrase "plus size polka dot wedding dress."

I scrolled and swiped and pinned. Then I gasped. I saw it.

This dress was everything I ever dreamed of and more.

It was retro, white with white polka dots, plenty of tulle, knee-length, fifties AF, and the woman wearing it was my kind of plus-size (as opposed to lots of plus-size wedding gowns that say they're plus, but only fit up to a size XL).

My heart was jumping for joy.

I became determined to use all my internet-sleuthing skills to find this dress. I sleuthed and sleuthed until I realized the obvious sleuth, which was just to click on the link of the picture. It took me to a blog based on rockabilly and retro style, and that particular post focused on a wedding.

I read the whole blog post, scanning each and every line, looking for a designer's name or a shop link. Then I read a phrase that broke my heart: The dress was custom-made for the bride.

My hopes were dashed. I couldn't buy one, I couldn't get lucky and snag one on eBay, I couldn't find one anywhere, because it simply didn't exist. It was hers. This dress was the ONLY dress of its kind.

The article did not have the couple's names, but I knew I had to find the bride. I saw that her sister had been her wedding planner, and the post gave her name. A bit more sleuthing, and I found the bride, Mary, on Facebook. Her profile picture was her in the damn dress.

I sent Mary a message. And it said something like this: "Hi, you don't know me. I promise I'm not a creeper or trying to scam you in any way, but I found you on Pinterest and I absolutely love your wedding dress and I'd love to buy it."

Now, Preston and I were NOT EVEN engaged. I was just so certain that this was the dress. I could tell from the first time I saw it. A few days later, miraculously, Mary answered. She had talked to her husband about it. Her husband said, "Well, you're not planning on needing it again, right?" She agreed.

A bit further down the line, we started to make plans for shipping and things. However, Mary lived in California, and at that time, California was experiencing one of its most destructive wildfires, causing devastation all over the state, and her neighborhood was being evacuated. Obviously, my dress was left behind as Mary and her family, thankfully, fled to safety.

Mary's family and house luckily were all safe in the fires, thank goodness, but the dress, when it arrived, it had been in storage and it had a few marks of wear and tear. It was beautiful, but it was definitely going to need some work. I was nervous it wasn't going to be salvageable for a wedding dress. I asked a friend who is a skilled costume designer (for real, she has designed costumes for celebs) to look at it, and she told me she would do her best but she couldn't promise. I was SO nervous.

Two days later, Amanda, the amazing CEO of Bombshell Bridal Boutique in St. Clair Shores, Michigan, outside Detroit, reached out to me and said she wanted to give me the full bridal experience. I accepted! It seemed like the perfect sign. There was no guarantee that my dream dress would work, and here was this UN-BELIEVABLE opportunity.

Now, I swear to Tim Hortons, Bombshell Bridal is staffed by a crew of angels. Every single person there was kind and funny and thoughtful and vibrant and genuine. After only two days, I seriously cried to have to say goodbye!

They had plus dresses in sizes ranging from 16 to 34 in the dang store! I had never been to a store where I could just try things on off the rack, have them fit, and have them available in a size up if I needed them. That kind of world hadn't really existed for me before then. I had never met a sales staff that I felt TRULY understood my needs and wanted me to find the exact right thing. While I was there, I found an amazing dress that was off-white with white polka dots and beyond gorgeous. It was comfortable and flattering and unique. It had some of the things that I loved about my first dress, and seemed like a pretty good fit! I was so excited to take it home.

My costume designer friend messaged me soon after to see if I wanted to try on the original, and said she thought she'd done enough to make it awesome. I met up with her to try it on, and when I heard the zipper close, I immediately started crying tears of joy. It felt like "the" dress.

Then I had two wedding dresses. Both equally gorgeous, and very totally me. They both had such fond memories and stories to tell with them. I debated what to do. I wanted to wear both.

With just weeks before the wedding, I still wasn't sure which dress I would be wearing.

I talked about it a lot and decided on a way that I could totally rock the Bombshell frock for the rehearsal dinner and still show off how unbelievably gorgeous it was. Then on our big day, I wore my original sleuth-worthy secondhand polka-dot dream wedding dress. I couldn't have planned it any better.

SIT UP, PULL UP, DRESS UP

"OH MY QUAD, BECKY. LOOK AT HER SQUATS."

So many people seem to think that plus-size people never work out, which is such a lie. Fun fact: As of this writing, I'm the heaviest I've ever been, and also the most physically active I've ever been. Clothing size or the number on the scale isn't a marker of whether someone is physically active.

My relationship with fitness, however, has a long and complicated history. Honestly, I HATE working out. I've been plus-size my entire life, despite consulting nutritionists, visiting hypnotists, buying into brand-name fad diets, getting gym memberships, and eating right. Managing my weight has always been difficult, and that played into my relationship with exercising. For most of my life, I always had one of two mindsets about working out: I was either doing it out of desperation, as part of a crash diet, working off double the calories I consumed in a day, pushing my body to the point of wear and tear, praying for the exercise to do something (anything) for my "problematic" body. Or I was pretending to myself and everyone around me that I loved working out, that I was a total gym rat, and making it part of my everyday routine was easy.

The truth is, I was neither desperate nor was it easy. While I do generally enjoy being physically active, I quickly get self-conscious during certain activities. I can't keep up on a hike before I'm huffing and puffing, and an elliptical can knock me into gasps in under seven minutes. And I've never really had an easy time facing these limitations. Even now, discussing my fitness shortcomings is usually a surefire way to get me to change the subject. Even writing this chapter, I feel a level of discomfort talking about this, but you're cool, so we'll get through it together.

For a few years in my mid-twenties, I stopped working out completely. Exercising felt like a punishment for my body. Years of being entrenched in corrupt beauty ideals made me believe my body wasn't good enough. A lifetime of watching television shows where teen girls think getting called "fat" is a huge insult, of seeing nonstop ads for gyms and "weight loss NOW," of standing to the side at the mall while my friends tried on jeans in stores with no sizes big enough for me, all made me feel less. The truth was, I was scared to exercise. I was bad at it. I'm still bad at it. I'm naturally clumsy, and I always felt out of sync with my own body. No one likes doing things they're bad at.

Eventually, I stopped going to the gym, letting my credit card be charged for using a facility I never even set foot inside. It made me feel like I had won against the judgments of random people talking about "fat girls at the gym walking slowly on the treadmill." They weren't talking about me, per se, but they could have been. So, by not working out, I wasn't being fat on a treadmill or going too slow. I wasn't living a cliché. I was content to be fat.

But I also didn't love being totally inactive. I missed the feeling of my body in motion. I missed feeling strong and healthy. I also didn't have to be doing it as a result of my relationship with my weight. My therapist completely normalized the idea that I didn't have to like it or be good at it to do it. That seemed radical to me, since I thought I was "supposed" to love it. She introduced the ideas that I didn't have to "work out" to exercise and didn't need to have any goals or benchmarks. I didn't have to be trying to lose weight: I could just go for a walk because it was a nice day. Doing or not doing a specific activity didn't have to assign any value to my body. With the help of my therapist, I was able to adjust my mindset to know that exercise could be a fun and regular part of my everyday routine.

I've gotten to the point in my relationship with exercise where I'm not trying to "get skinny," but instead trying to actually learn how to enjoy physical activities, and in the process, learn which ones I like and which I don't like. I like taking long walks with my dog, Charlie. I love to swim all summer long, in any type of water. I like to go to the gym with my husband for an hour-long workout, a mix of cardio and strength training.

Now, I openly despise stair climbers. I am convinced that they're the devil in exercise-equipment form. A nice morning run? Yeah, I hate that, too. But I've learned that I don't need to use a climber or run a marathon—there's no reason to! I can be active and enjoy myself in other ways. It's still a process, but I'm learning to love exercise again.

Like every activity we love in life, I quickly realized I needed the proper attire in order to do it right. So the very first thing I did on my journey to reconnect with exercise was buy myself a really good pair of shoes.

Yup. That's right. Shoes.

I had loathed the chunky-white, extra-wide dad sneakers I had been forced to wear for gym during high school. During college, my little white canvas sneakers with zero arch support were more fashionable, but definitely not practical for workouts. I bought myself my first pair of sturdy and cute athletic sneakers as an adult.

My beloved Oscar and Javier: my favorite shoes, ever.

And let me tell you: They changed my dang life. It didn't hurt to work out anymore. They made my walks with Charlie seem not so long, and hitting the gym didn't leave my feet and legs and hips aching.

Good shoes were all it took to kick-start my relationship with exercise. My shoes had such a good impact on me that I named them. (I'm one of those weird people who names everything from my car to my toaster.) And Oscar and Javier have yet to let me down!

Sweatin' in Style

As I started feeling more at ease while being active, I learned what types of clothing I needed to wear to stay safe and comfortable. When I realized that I was getting that chub-rub burn on my inner thighs on long walks, I swapped my ratty old shorts for either great performance leggings or sturdy shorts designed to be durable with friction. I realized that the oversize tee I was wearing was scratching my neck and making me feel bulky and gross. So I swapped it out for a cute and more fitted top. These small but important clothing changes finally made me feel confident and comfortable with being active.

To get you started on your own fitness journey, here's a list of my must-have exercise pieces!

1. Discover your very own Oscar & Javier.

Get yourself a great pair of athletic shoes. Find some that are the right size and width, and that offer great arch support, in a style and color you love! If you're not sure of your proper shoe size, try going to a shoe store and getting a fitting.

2. Dress yo'self!

You don't need to be runway-ready to hit the gym, the trails, or the sidewalks. But you should wear clothes that fit you properly and that you feel good wearing!

3. Dress yo'self (part 2)!

Your clothes should be appropriate for your activity. This seems so obvious, but I still see people going for runs in baggy sweatshirts when it's 75 degrees and sunny. You don't need to cover up or hide while working out. Use common sense to figure out what's appropriate to wear.

4. Does your bra even lift, girl?

Because it should. Find a great sports bra that is supportive and breathable, and that fits properly. If you can't keep your ladies in place, you're cruising for a black eye when one goes rogue and smacks you in the face. I might be speaking from personal experience on that one.

5. Ponytail as old as time.

You don't want your hair flopping in your face or getting stuck to your sweaty brow or neck. Stock up on clips and hair elastics. If you have bangs, find a great washable headband!

6. Headphones & a phone holder.

Whether you're a phone-in-your-pocket, -waistband, -armband, or -hand type, and whether you're a killer-playlist, audiobook, or podcast person—you're probably listening to something! So make sure your headphones are comfortable and your phone is secure and not going to go flying during a jumping jack.

Let's get physical.

Some Ideas for Incorporating Exercise into Your Daily Life

It's easy to say all that, but I've sat in my car, all dressed and ready to go into the gym, and turned around and drove home because I was nervous about exercising in public as a plus-size woman. It took a lot of time to grit my teeth and realize that no one was looking at me as judgmentally as I feared. As much as the outfit can change your mindset, it doesn't get rid of anxiety or stress or fear. As you start on your exercise journey, especially if you haven't had the healthiest relationship with exercise before, I wanted to offer you a few "low-risk" activities to get yourself more comfortable with moving!

- Park farther away from your destination and get in some extra steps.
- Double how often you walk your dog.
- Do squats or stretches during smaller moments of downtime, like when you're waiting for water to boil or for the shower to get hot. Do some jumping jacks while you heat something up in the microwave.

- Lunge your way to the mailbox (even if it feels silly!).
- Learn a few basic yoga poses that you can do for five minutes every day (Downward-Facing Dog, Cobra Pose, and Child's Pose are some of my daily go-tos).
- Get a jump rope and get your heart rate going in your garage for a few minutes a day.
- Learn the "Single Ladies" choreography and work it into your getting-ready routine. (All hail Queen Bey.)
- Start with one sit-up. Do two the next day. Then three the next, and so on. Slow and steady wins the race!
- Tread water in the deep end of the pool for a few minutes next time you go swimming.
- Play Twister at your next game night.
- Take the stairs sometimes.
- Utilize the health apps on your phone and see how many steps you take on average in a day, then set a goal to beat that.
- Help a friend move. (You'll earn bonus friendship points!)

Remember:

- If you're still healing from a conflicted journey with working out, keep on healing. There's no rush.
- If you feel pressure to exercise, ask yourself why you feel that way and answer yourself honestly.
- You can get active gradually! Don't feel pressure to rush in at once.
- Get yourself a great pair of athletic sneakers.
- Find an activity that you like, and keep going!

RECLAIMING SATURN

HELLO, MY NAME IS ABBY, AND I AM A RECOVERING THEATRE KID.
I was that teen with stage makeup, in a cast T-shirt, singing at a table filled with twenty kids exactly like me at the local Applebee's. I paced up and down the band wing waiting for the cast list. I watched *Glee*. I lived to say things like "I can't, I have rehearsal" or "What do you mean you don't know who Kristin Chenoweth is?" I had character shoes in every color. I was annoying and I thrived.

When I was in seventh grade, I was in a production of *Schoolhouse Rock Live! Jr.* The play was probably a solid seventy minutes long and had a cast of a dozen thirteen-year-olds. It was directed by an eighth-grade English teacher who also coached field hockey. It was not high-stakes theatre. But for us, the zitty and brace-faced middle school theatre kids, it might as well have been Broadway.

NOT-SO-ITSY-BITSY TEENIE-WEENIE YELLOW POLKA-DOT BIKINI

WEAR THE SWIMSUIT. That's it. That's my main advice when it comes to beach and pool attire. Just wear it. If you choose to remember only one sentence in this book, please let it be: Wear the dang swimsuit.

I would argue that wearing a swimsuit is something many people struggle to feel comfortable with. I have a friend who is a size 2 who will only wear shorts and a sports bra. I have another friend who fits into a size small bikini, but only wears gym shorts and T-shirts when swimming in a lake.

When I was in middle and high school, I usually felt like I could tell how another girl felt about their body based on how she reacted during the swimming requirement for gym class. The really confident ones just got naked like it was nothing and left the rest of us with our eyes permanently glued to the ground, as we tried to not stare with sheer amazement that someone could feel okay doing that. Then there were the stall girls, who changed in the cramped little bathroom stalls. (We support bodily autonomy whatever it looks like. No judging the stall girls.) There were the girls who wore their swimsuit to school under their clothes to avoid changing. Then there were girls like me, who changed with their back to the group as fast as humanly possible, to avoid the attention that the other three options drew.

I remember when my girlfriends stopped swimming because they couldn't stand the thought of their legs being seen or their tummies jiggling.

I remember at fourteen feeling utterly confused at the beach when a boy my own age told me I looked like a beached whale. That same day, a man old enough to be my father told me I looked sexy. What is a teenager supposed to glean from those two pieces of feedback? The answer: Nothing—neither of those men had any right to make those comments.

Beach body anxiety doesn't care what size you are or what you actually look like. Beach body anxiety doesn't care how many squats you've done. Beach body anxiety does, however, care deeply about that thing your mom said to you in seventh grade. Beach body anxiety cares deeply about that thing Jessica M. said on the eighth-grade field trip to the water park.

Beach body anxiety, it turns out, is a huge butthead.

Honestly, what is it about going to the beach that can knock a confident person to their knees with paralysis? When did we all decide that wearing a garment appropriate for a set activity would be the thing that kept us up at night?

Double honestly, your beach body anxiety probably isn't your fault. Starting in March (every year, without fail), promotions and ads start appearing for diets and workouts to help you get a "beach body." Maybe it's all the email newsletters that promote the return to the gym as getting "bikini ready." Maybe it's all our moms, who were raised with painful beauty standards by their own weight-obsessed mothers. Maybe it's the trillion-dollar beauty industrial complex. Who knows?

I have a couple of spoiler alerts here.

If your body is at the beach, it is a beach body.

Really, think about it. Logically, if your body is at the beach, then it is a beach body. You can start your internal retraining with that idea. Based on solid reason alone, any body on a beach qualifies as a beach body. Sometimes that piece of logic is all it takes to get us to put on that swimsuit and tell our inner insecure little kid to shut up.

If they make bikinis in your size, then you have a bikini body.

Do yourself a favor and make a switch here. Change the phrase "I don't have a bikini body" to "I am actively choosing to not wear a bikini," because that's more accurate. Clothing manufacturers make bikinis in almost every size. If they make it in your size, you can wear it. You're the only person stopping yourself from putting one on.

Swimsuits are uniforms.

You wear running shoes to run. You wear pajamas while you sleep. You wear coats in the cold, rain boots in the rain, and ugly sweaters to office holiday parties. Therefore, you should wear a swimsuit to the beach. It's just the most pragmatic choice of outfit for the activity.

Swimsuits are the least brave thing you can wear at the beach.

Stop saying that people wearing swimsuits are brave. Even if it's meant as a compliment, it's a polarizing statement. Wearing the appropriate garment for the appropriate activity isn't brave. Emergency room doctors are brave. The only way wearing a swimsuit is an act of bravery is if I have a dragon-slaying sword tucked somewhere in my tankini, which I can assure you I do not.

There was an episode of an early-2000s sitcom that I absolutely loved as a kid (and still do) that posed three main female characters as being desperate to be beach body ready. The first woman actually gets liposuction just so she can go to the beach. The second woman starves herself to the point of feeling faint. The third woman (who had given birth recently) is shamed for wearing a practical one-piece. Watching the episode now is almost nauseating.

Because, I'm sorry. What is the moral of that story? That the sexiness of a bathing suit is its most important quality? That you need to get surgery or make yourself sick to look sexy at the beach? That even if you've just given birth, your body needs to get back into beach-worthy shape ASAP? Don't get me wrong—it's still one of my favorite shows. But that narrative is definitely dated. It's time to change the story. You need to be your own Eliza Schuyler, put yourself back in the narrative, and wear the dang swimsuit.

You don't have to "earn" wearing a two-piece!

Bikini Buzzwords

For those times that you're not feeling like the "bad beach" you truly are, try remembering some of these bikini buzzwords.

ROOM: Remember, you're trying on swimsuits in dressing rooms with fluorescent lights, no tan or freckles from the sun, and if you're anything like me, you usually still have your granny panties on for hygiene. Literally no one looks good like that except for Chrissy Teigen, who is a literal goddess. Reflect on the room, not your rump.

CAN'T: During choreography rehearsals for my high school musicals, if we ever said we couldn't do something, we had to do ten push-ups. "Can't" usually meant we just hadn't yet or were choosing not to try. Retrain your brain to know who is saying you can't wear that cute suit. (Newsflash: It's you.)

BRAVE: You're not brave for wearing a swimsuit. Stop telling people they're brave for wearing a swimsuit. Stop your brain from even thinking it.

REQUIRED: To swim, you need a swimsuit. Plain and simple. If anyone gives you grief about your suit, remember it's a utility garment.

LITERALLY: Literally no one is looking at you or thinking about you as much as you're thinking about you. Just wear the dang swimsuit.

THRIFT
STORE CHIC

MUCH LIKE MACKLEMORE, I have had more than one time in my life when I only had twenty dollars in my pocket but wanted to be stunning. However, it was less than effing awesome. I *lovelovelove* thrift store shopping. It's not only a way to introduce an element of sustainability to your fashion, but it's downright fun.

I love walking into a thrift shop and seeing what vintage relics or hidden gems I can find. My very first toe dip into the fashion pond was when I graduated from college and had $90 to my name and suddenly needed a business-y wardrobe. I didn't even own a skirt. After spotting a pair of black pants that would wipe out a third of my budget, well, I knew I needed to hit the thrift shops.

The first day I went out thrifting, I ended up with a haul that was pretty mismatched but it was what I could afford. It was a big risk, but I decided I could wear those pieces with a few things I already had. That haul ended up being what I started using for #OOTD pictures and was the very first step of launching *The Penny Darling*.

When it comes to plus-size thrifting, a few plus-specific challenges present themselves. For example, plus-size fashion is relatively new. Even when I was a teen, I was relegated to frumpy grandma sweaters, shapeless dresses, and out-of-style jeans from the department store. Cute plus-size vintage or thrifted clothing is a little rarer of a gem, because there's simply less of it. But never fear, there are a few tricks to making sure someone else's trash becomes your treasure.

1. Try stuff on even if it's not your size.

Don't worry about size. Women's sizes are jerks and vary wildly. Friends, we've talked about this. I have stuff ranging from sizes 16 to 30 and medium to 6X. Just try it on. For $4, you can afford to try it on.

2. Try stuff on even if it's not your style.

It may look like something you would NEVER wear, but match it with the right shoes/pants/top, and it could be a really cool statement piece. Sometimes it's unique! Just try it on. Again, for $4, you can afford to.

3. Look at whatcha got first.

Sometimes it's really helpful to look at that awesome top or weird-colored skirt hanging in the back of your closet that you haven't found the right matching piece for. Sometimes it helps to think, *I really need a red cardigan to match this dress*, or, *That weird silver skirt would look great with a jewel-tone top*. A family friend always asks us to tell her what we're looking for if she's doing a big ol' thrift haul because she *needs* to have something to look for.

4. Rewardrobe.

That was an attempt at a portmanteau of "reward" and "wardrobe." How did I do? Anyway, lots of thrift stores and secondhand shops have special sale programs. I know some that have a 50 percent discount on Wednesdays, some that have a reward points system to earn dollars off your next purchase, and some that give a discount if you donate! Be sure to check your local stores to see what deals you might be able to snag.

5. Wear clothes you might match potential purchases with.

I like to wear black leggings and a black scoop-neck top to go thrifting. I have a lot of clothes that are cut similarly to those pieces. If a thrifted top works with my black leggings, then it will likely work with my other leggings, too!

6. What is your damage, Heather?

Sometimes the buttons might be a bit loose, there might be minor pilling or loose threads, or it's a little bit dirty. But if it's $5 and you think it's worth your time and effort, then buy it, babes! If you're quick at hemming skirts or taking in dresses, buy it. But only if you know you're willing to do the work. Now, I am not a good seamstress. So if I'll have to shorten or alter something, I tend to shy away, unless I know someone will help me out (I'm looking at you, Mom). Be realistic about if you're *actually* going to alter or clean it.

7. Don't be duped by a deal.

It's really easy to want to buy fifteen tops for $30, but you probably don't want or need fifteen tops. And they probably aren't all great. Pick out a set number of items that you're willing to take home. I have the worst habit of saying, "Oh, it's only a few bucks, I should just get it," so I always set a limit for myself.

8. Rank & conquer.

After hitting a few of your local thrift shops, take note of which places are likely to have the best goods in each category. For example, remember which has the best clothes, the quirkiest home goods section, the sketchiest bin of shoes, etc. I have one favorite place for cool art and vintage housewares and another favorite that tends to have the best plus size selection.

9. To every season, turn, turn, turn.

Experience has taught me that the best time to thrift is mid-fall (late October/ early November) and early summer (May/ June). That's when people tend to clean out the clothes they didn't wear the previous season. In the fall, people are getting rid of all their summer clothes, and in the spring, people are clearing out all the sweaters and coats they accumulated over the winter. Yes, that does mean it's easier to shop off season, but honestly, who cares? If you have to wait a few months to wear a sweater, but you love it and it's cheap, then it's worth it. I've found designer summer dresses for $5 in February and high-end coats for sale in the middle of summer. They were worth waiting to wear.

10. It's more than just clothes.

Thrifting is economical, sustainable, and fun. Why stop at clothes? I got my coffee table, about half my wall art, my Christmas tree, some purses, a picnic basket, a utensil holder, a retro yellow phone, a lamp, and even vases for my wedding flowers all at secondhand shops. Utilize what's there.

11. Hopefully not sporadically.

The stock at a thrift store changes almost daily, and people donate stuff weekly. You can usually ask what day they restock with new donations. So if you strike out, don't worry! Go again in a week or two and see what's rotated in.

12. Get creative.

A wicker purse can be a great way to make a Red Riding Hood–chic outfit. And sometimes, you can find some mismatched pajama tops that can be repurposed with a skirt. Or you might spot a neat bookshelf that you could varnish and make look brand-new. Maybe you see a vintage suitcase that could be a cute side table. Just be open-minded as to what an item could be (and your level of skill with DIY). Since I'm a theatre person, I often buy vintage pieces in my size for future costumes.

IT'S JUST A BUNCH OF HOCUS-POCUS

AH, HALLOWEEN. A day for eating tons of "fun"-size chocolate bars, telling ghost stories, having virgins light the Black Flame Candle (or at least, per *Hocus Pocus*), and getting both tricked and treated. Or, if you're a grown-up, it's a day for having your doorbell constantly rung until you turn off your porch light, put out a bowl of candy, and hit a bar.

I LOVE Halloween. (Actually, I think I'm obsessed with holidays in general, but I love each one for a different reason.) There are so many great things about Halloween, but most of all, I'm enamored with the costumes. As you know, I've spent a lot of time in theatre, so costume curating has always been an activity where I shine. I remember once some school friends were filming a short film (as theatre kids are prone to do on the weekends for YouTube series that never get finished). As they were talking to me, they kept listing some seemingly random things that they needed, like, "We need a tiara. We need a sailor's hat. We need oversize sunglasses. We need a wicker basket." And I had every single one of those in my car. So yeah, costumes are sort of my thing.

Now, I know that most people aren't as into glitz and glamour as I am. But if you've ever been to a Halloween party or participated in an elementary school pageant, or even just if you follow Neil Patrick Harris on Instagram (if you don't already, you really should), you know that what qualifies as a costume can range from a T-shirt to full Met Gala–style creations.

But with so much range and so many different ways to go, where do you even start? Deciding on a costume can definitely feel overwhelming, so I've got some pro tips to help. Grab your pillowcase, map out your candy route, and let's talk about ways you can get treated, not tricked, the next time you're getting your spooky on!

The tenth Doctor and the TARDIS

1. Couples costumes are not lame.

Or at least, I don't think they are! I think getting to go as a famous duo is one of those unexpected perks of having a significant other. It's kind of like when you're in high school or college and you go with your squad as the Ninja Turtles. (Because who has ever seen one Ninja Turtle out on Halloween? . . . Well, not when you're in college, anyway!) And really, when it comes down to it, you and your S.O. are just a smaller squad. Preston and I have done Mary Poppins and Bert, Alice and the Mad Hatter, Mickey and Minnie, Doctor Who and the TARDIS, and other fun pop culture duos. I've also seen some cute peanut-butter-and-jelly costumes! So don't let people tell you it's dorky. Get your duo on! If it's really not your thing, that's perfectly okay, too. Don't let anyone pressure you on Halloween.

2. Costumes can & should be fairly inexpensive.

Now, I truly DO NOT understand why anyone who is not a celebrity (like Heidi Klum, who obviously has some disposable income) would choose to spend a fortune on Halloween costumes. I just don't. Wear something comparable to what whoever you're trying to "be" wears, and even if it's not spot-on, people will get the idea. If you're going as a Disney princess, for instance, you don't need a full-length, detailed, period-appropriate gown. To look the part of Snow White, you really just need a yellow skirt, a navy top, and a red hair bow.

There's no need to go crazy when planning out costumes. A lot can be found in thrift stores, your parents' attic, or the back of your closet. It's really doable. When I was kid, my mom bought an old ballet tutu from a garage sale and made me little frilly tulle ears, and I went as a poodle. The whole thing cost less than $10.

3. DIY is DI-YAY!

Building on the cost-efficiency theme, it's pretty quick and easy to alter your own clothes and incorporate other elements using some scissors and easy-to-remove glue.

One of my proudest DIY-costume moments was during college when my friend decided to have a toga party. It was January. There was two feet of snow on the ground. And much like a sitcom middle schooler who is supposed to make three dozen cupcakes for the bake sale, I forgot all about it until the night of the party. I was like, *Oh no! I was supposed to do something toga-y.*

Never one to miss a costumed affair, I pulled out a pair of white shorts and a ruffled white shirt, and tied a long scarf into a loop to be a sash. I cut the leaves off the fake flowers in my room with a butter knife, then superglued them to a headband, all about an hour before I went to the party.

4. You should tone it down for work.

I used to work in a theatre, and weirdly, no one there got dressed up for Halloween. The guy I shared an office with seriously just safety-pinned a cotton ball to the waistband of his jeans and said, "Now I'm a bunny."

However, adding a pair of animal ears, a witch's hat, or a crown to an existing outfit is super appropriate for an office setting. It's subtle, but still on-theme. (Now, obviously, if you're a teacher and your administration allows it, I encourage you to get on with your bad self and dress up with your students.) When it comes to dressing up at work, my rule of thumb is that you should be able to look like you're not wearing a costume in under five minutes. In other words, your costume should be easy to take off if you're called into a last-second important meeting.

5. Don't feel bad about getting your slut on.

As the great Cady Heron once said, "Halloween is the one night a year when a girl can dress like a total slut and no other girls can say anything about it."

As long as the setting is appropriate (i.e., not work or a kids' costume party), no one should make you feel bad about wearing whatever you want and embracing your sexuality. Don't let anyone shame you and tell you that you're the wrong size, race, or gender to wear something sexy. (I mean, I wouldn't recommend wearing anything that's going to get you arrested or that makes going to the bathroom impossible, but that's just me.)

One college Halloween, I saw a girl dressed as a sexy ghost. She had a sheet over her head, but she had cut the sides off so you could see her bikini underneath. I appreciate the effort, ghoulfriend! She didn't let anyone stop her, and neither should you.

6. Your main goal should be to have fun!

On Halloween, channel your inner child and just go have a good time. Don't buy an expensive costume for the wrong reasons.

Instead, put together a fun and easy costume, and enjoy the night.

While I advocate that you should wear whatever you want, I STRONGLY advise you not to wear high heels. You might be walking long distances outside in the dark while trick-or-treating, or you might be drinking alcohol, and both of those are TERRIBLE to do while you're stumbling around in heels.

So on Halloween, get your squad together—whoever that may be—and hit the streets for treats and the bar for some tricks. Or head to the house of that one friend who is always willing to have the party! Take lots of pictures, enjoy yourself, and make sure you have a safe way to get home. Stay spooky!

SLAY VS. SLEIGH

ME, ELEVEN MONTHS OF THE YEAR: SLAY.

Me, in December: Sleigh.

Happy Holidays!

Merry Christmas!

Happy Kwanzaa!

Happy Hanukkah!

Merry Winter Solstice!

Season's Greetings!

Happy or Merry Winter-Holiday-You-Celebrate-That-Is-Underrepresented-in-Mainstream-Culture!

Whatever it is you're doing this winter, the question always remains, *What the heck do I wear to my holiday gathering?* Then the next question is usually, *What do I give as gifts?*

Now, when it comes to holiday gatherings, why is it always approximately −5 degrees outside and approximately 95 degrees in your relatives' houses? (Yes, this is VERY exact science, thank you for noticing.) I'm one of those people who is always too hot. I'm just as hot in December as I am in July. Which means that for me and other temperature-challenged folks like myself, dressing for holiday gatherings is always tricky, because you don't want to show up in a sundress while it's snowing, even if it's Bahama temps in your aunt's living room.

Furthermore, when deciding on your holiday outfit, there's approximately one million questions to ask yourself. Are there kids or pets you'll have to be moving around? I don't wear black to my in-laws' because there are literally nine cats there and I'd leave looking Andrew Lloyd Webber–chic. Is it more of a casual occasion, where most people will have jeans on? Is it fancy? Will you have to, at any point, sit on the floor? Because donning a miniskirt is going to turn sitting around the tree into an Olympic activity. Are you going to be eating a ton so you'll need an outfit that can breathe? Is there a religious gathering involved? Is this a party with friends? The office holiday party? Are you expected to help cook or play with the kids? When I was a kid, I used to play with my boy cousins, so nothing too fancy was going to work because I needed some agility for the inevitable Nerf gunfight that was bound to break out.

And since you just spent two whole car payments buying people gifts because you love them, you probably don't want to wear an outfit that's going to break the bank. You want to feel festive, merry, and bright, not hot, uncomfortable, and broke all day and night. I have worn one too many itchy sweaters and regretted it when someone cranked the heat up in the car on the way (over the river and through the woods) to Grandma's.

The first Christmas I spent with my in-laws, my mother-in-law insisted that we show up at nine a.m. in our "Christmas jammies" (which the "jammie elf" had dropped off for us ahead of time) and bring a change of clothes for later in the day. We drove over an hour in our jammies to wear them for one hour. That happened exactly once before I said, "No thanks, Tom Hanks," the next year. Now that we're married, we spend Christmas morning in comfy jammies we gift each other instead.

Wherever you're going or whatever you're celebrating, there's one tip that will always apply and I cannot stress enough: Wear layers. Please, for the love of Dasher and Dancer, wear layers. Most of my Christmases growing up started with lighting luminarias (freezing), rehearsing my Christmas pageant (warm), going to church (way too warm), going back to my grandparents' house (approximately 900 degrees), heading outside to play with my cousins (literally freezing because it was nighttime in winter), and opening presents around the tree (when I was a kid, I couldn't focus on the temperature during this part, but it was probably super warm). So layer up. Add sweaters, jackets, scarves, and shoes that are easy to transition from a stuffy kids' pageant to caroling door to door.

But aside from layering, what in the North Pole should you wear?

My Santa-bae.

It's the Twelve Advices of Christmas

Obviously, you know your budget, family, religious traditions, and plans for your holiday soiree best, so I trust you to make choices that work for you—but here are some tips that work in general.

1.

DON'T SPEND ALL YOUR MONEY ON TACKY SWEATERS. Those stoned-looking llamas in Santa hats are funny for your office party once. No need to blow a whole paycheck. Make a great donation to a holiday toy drive instead.

2.

IF YOU AIM FOR GETTING "WINTER PIECES" AS OPPOSED TO "HOLIDAY PIECES," you can utilize them a few more months of the year, which is a bonus for your wardrobe ROI, which, as a savings queen, I always appreciate.

3.

DON'T BUY SUPER-THICK SWEATERS FOR INDOOR EVENTS with seventeen relatives and every appliance going full gear. You'll be hot. There's no world where your aunt Diane didn't anticipate everyone being in the kitchen and then opened the back door so it's either sweltering or freezing depending on where you're standing.

4.

THE ACTIVITY MATTERS. Dressing for a day out sledding versus going to church requires totally different wardrobe options.

5.

IF YOU'RE DOING ANYTHING INVOLVING SNOW, BRING A COMPLETE CHANGE OF CLOTHING. Bring a change all the way down to your socks and underpants. Nothing sucks more than having to spend the rest of the day with wet undies or leggings because you didn't plan ahead.

6.

BONUS SNOW TIP: Layering a few pairs of thick leggings is a decent alternative to snowpants for light snow activity (like a snowball fight or sledding).

7.

IF YOU WEAR ANYTHING SLEEVELESS WITH SEQUINS, the sequins will totally cut up your underarms and it will hurt "like a sonofabitch" (as my Pennsylvania Dutch grandpa was prone to saying at Christmas gatherings).

8.

IF YOU'RE GOING TO BE IN ANY SHARED-BATHROOM SITUATION, YOU MIGHT WANT TO SKIP THE TIGHTS. When you're out Christmas caroling and you stop to pee, if you have to finagle your tights up in a porta-potty, your carol crew is going to get the elf outta there, and you'll be sweaty and swearing and seven houses behind by the time you get them back up.

9.

I TOTALLY SUPPORT MATCHING JAMMIES WITH YOUR FAMILY. Preston and I (and our dog, Charlie) love wearing matching Christmas jammies.

10.

I ALSO TOTALLY SUPPORT BEING A HOLIDAY DORK. There is a wholesome fun to loving holidays that's hard to beat. Buy a dress that makes you look like a snowman. Decorate your tree in November. Wear the reindeer ears and the dreidel sweater! Embrace your inner Cindy-Lou Who.

11.

YOU ARE TOTALLY ALLOWED TO EAT WHATEVER YOU WANT ON THANKSGIVING AND CHRISTMAS AND ALL HOLIDAYS WITHOUT HAVING TO MAKE EXCUSES. You don't need to mention breaking your diet or cheating when you eat a piece of cheesecake, or talk about how you haven't eaten all day to justify eating a meal. Take diet and diet conversation out of your holiday meal prep, and eat the cookies. You're not going to remember the calories you saved, but you will remember the tradition of baking with your niece or your favorite aunt.

12.

DON'T GIVE PEOPLE CLOTHING AS A GIFT UNLESS YOU KNOW THEY WANT SOMETHING SPECIFICALLY IN A CERTAIN SIZE. There's nothing more awkward than guessing wrong and making someone feel self-conscious.

I have always been a total holiday dork. I wrap every gift individually. I have my tree up by the middle of November. I sacrifice way too much storage space in my closets for decorations. (Hey, you try storing a six-foot tree in a two-bedroom apartment with exactly three closets.) I have a full bin of clothing dedicated to candy-cane leggings and Fair Isle sweaters.

And since this is the holiday-themed chapter, I want to end it with a piece of coal: a hilarious story.

I used to participate in Christmas pageants at our local church. I'm not a particularly religious person, but I was very involved with my church youth program because they put on youth plays. Every Christmas Eve, there was a musical during the evening service. They were twenty-minute, cheesy, ordered-from-a-catalog musicals that we performed in place of a sermon. Being a true theatre kid, I saw every single performance as an opportunity to shine, even if it was to captive neighbors who did not sign up to see a musical performed by children at church. Honestly, children's theatre does deserve a warning to audience members. I would now like to tell you some things I remember from these musical masterpieces.

One of them was called *Twas the Last Mailing Day Before Christmas*, and I have no memory of it at all except that the entire play took place in the line at the post office.

In a different production called *Mayhem in Bethlehem* (whose main character was named Noah Lott, and which had a "Randy Looney" as an Andy Rooney type), I played a news reporter named Vesta Gates, and my best friend played a character named Lorna Limelight who had to faint into my arms. And one night I missed and dropped her like a sack of potatoes, and I laughed so hard I cried.

In one play that I could not tell you the name of to save my life, I played a character named Fern, a Christmas tree activist protesting people buying trees in a parking lot.

There was one masterpiece called *Christmas at Bethlehem Gulch* that featured a real song titled "Baa Baa Better Believe" and we *baa*-ed for two minutes to represent Jesus as the Lamb of God.

Our director treated every show like a Broadway-caliber performance, and one year threw his conducting baton (he was conducting to a CD of synth music) into the Nativity scene at the front of the church.

One year, I knocked over a bottle of wine as I was trying to change my costume in the sacristy, and my "good black skirt" smelled like red wine for months.

In one of these masterpieces, I played a thorn. I wore a brown sweatsuit covered in ill-placed, brown-spray-painted foam cones that looked more like a Madonna bra than a thorn costume.

One year, a girl playing a character literally named "Socialite" threw up onstage but didn't leave. We appreciate that kind of commitment to a performance.

One year, the girl playing Mary in the Nativity scene dropped the Baby Jesus doll, which was actually a Cabbage Patch Kid from the Sunday School room. This went over particularly poorly.

My friend and I choreographed one of these musicals. We misheard the lyric "star of wonder, star of night" as "star of wonder, star of might," so we choreographed everyone to make bodybuilder poses, which made no sense with the actual lyrics.

One of the plays was called *The Christmas S.O.C.C.E.R. Team* (*S.O.C.C.E.R.* stood for "Society of Christmas Carolers Emergency Rescue").

One year we caught some people hooking up in the sanctuary, because the cliché of "sexually active band geeks" that *Mean Girls* described is doubled for theatre kids, and not even the Holy Spirit can quench that.

Bonus: The Twenty-Fifth Advice of Tip-Mas

When it comes to awesome gift giving, here's my not-so-patented formula for choosing a gift that's a guaranteed total showstopper. I don't mean to brag (okay, yes, I actually do), but I have made someone cry from a thoughtful gift under the Christmas tree for four years straight. I'm very good.

So this is the perfect recipe:

2 parts practical × 1 part personal + your budget = perfect gift

I like to think of something that the person needs or will utilize frequently, add a personal touch, and then minus my budget. Here's an example: One year I knew my brother needed new headphones. I searched far and wide to find him some *Back to the Future* headphones (he's totally obsessed), and they were within my budget. During the pandemic Christmas, when Broadway was shut down, I bought every DVD of live-filmed productions to gift to Preston. A friend who was getting married got a gift card to the company that would be doing her wedding invitations, along with a roll of stamps.

And remember, you can have the best outfit and the best gift in the whole town, but *The Grinch* taught us that Christmas means a bit more. Embrace leaving the cookies out. Remember to take extra time around the holidays for the people you love, people in need, and the magic and joy the holidays tend to bring.

DESIGNER OR DUPE?

FASHION CAN BE A LITTLE (or totally, actually) all over the map when it comes to price. Nearly identical pieces of clothing can cost insanely different amounts. So how do you decide when it's worth it to splurge on that awesome tank you love, or when to buy the cheap knockoff instead?

Your girl is a SAVE queen. I am all about coupons and deals and discounts and inexpensive finds. I am a sale fiend—I get pumped by just the idea of a great sale and kind of treat it like a competitive sport. I used to think that when it came to clothes, the cheaper, the better. Hell, I still brag that one Black Friday, I scored seventeen identical V-neck T-shirts in seventeen different colors for about $12. It's one of my proudest hauls! And as you know, I actually got my start on Instagram by posting items I got at the thrift store for my first big-girl job. However, like most things that I did in my early twenties, I was wrong about buying everything on the cheap. (Don't tell my mom I admitted that.)

10 Staples to Splurge On

1. Two great pairs of jeans: one medium wash, one dark wash.

Denim is versatile and easy to wear, and has basically never gone out of style since the 1950s. I recommend getting a medium wash for casual looks and a dark wash for more formal looks. You'll wear and wash them a ton, so make sure they are made to last.

2. Really supportive athletic shoes.

If I spend too much time without arch support on a long walk or a run, my feet hurt for days afterward! Sturdy athletic shoes are really important for your overall posture, gait, and health—so make sure that you spend accordingly.

3. Neutral-colored winter coat.

This one is easy. If you live in a climate that requires a cold-weather coat, invest in a good one. A classic wool, leather, or down coat is definitely an item on which to splurge. Much like Justin Timberlake, I prefer my tips frosted, not my fingertips!

4. A great blazer.

Honestly, even if you're not an office worker, it's still good to have one in your wardrobe. A blazer is a versatile piece that can dress up a pair of jeans, add a professional edge to a favorite dress, or even be styled for brunch with flowy shorts!

5. Sturdy backpack.

This might seem odd, but a great backpack has saved my butt more than once. I especially use them when I fly (it's so much easier getting my ticket and ID out when my hands are free). A backpack is great for overnight travel, hitting the gym, hiking, camping, adventures—it has endless versatility and durability! Seriously, my mom bought me a durable backpack as a little kid and I carried it from my first day of kindergarten to my last day of college. No joke, you can really get your money's worth from a good backpack.

6. A purse that you'll carry everywhere.

I am prone to having, like, seven purses in rotation, and I end up forgetting things in some of them, or they get damaged or dirty and wear out quick. I started spending a few extra dollars to get a quality purse, and they last so much longer. Learn from my mistakes and invest in a sturdy, versatile purse.

7. A black dress.

An office party? A wedding? A funeral? A work function? A happy hour? A job interview? A first date? Adding ears for a Halloween costume? (I see you, Karen.) A little black dress can go a lonnnnng way, so get a great one that you love.

8. Neutral heels or other office shoes.

Again, great shoes can carry you a long way, metaphorically and physically. You spend more of your time in your work shoes than any other shoes you own, so make sure they're good quality.

9. Supportive bras.

You probably wear a bra most days, and it can be killer uncomfortable if it's a bad one. No one likes getting poked with errant wires or pinched by weird cups. So (wo)man up and get a few really good bras.

10. Something you really love!

You should have something in your closet that you just LOVE. Every once in a while, it's worth it to "treat yo'self." A hot-pink moto jacket? Splurge. A cool tutu? Splurge. A funky red dress? Oh heck yes, splurge!

Save

On the flip side, there are lots of things that are NOT worth spending half a paycheck on! These items are the ones you buy thrifted and inexpensive, or even borrow if you can.

As much as your girl LOVES Halloween, you shouldn't be dropping a bunch of money on a costume that you'll wear for one party. No one needs to be dressed as a Sexy Nun or Sexy Corn in general, let alone with a high price tag! You also don't need to spend money on a T-shirt or a blouse you can only wear every once in a while. Again, it's all about utility!

Since I already gave you my recommended splurge list, I honestly endorse trying to save on most everything else. By its very nature, fashion is fluid and changes fast. It's an industry that thrives on being as up-to-the-minute as possible. So don't get caught up in spending a lot on something that's super trendy. You don't want to be the 1980s girl who spent BIG MONEY on plastic pumps with live goldfish in them only for them to be out of style in a month . . . or a week.

Here's my list of where you can cut cost corners in your wardrobe!

1. Tees & tanks.

Graphic tees, layering tanks, camisoles, and classic white T-shirts are places where you can scrimp. You'll end up wearing them under sweaters or with shorts in the summer, and will cycle through several of each kind. No need to #spendspendspend on something you could buy in a pack of ten and likely get the same quality.

2. Sunglasses.

You're probably going to drop them off the side of a canoe, leave them at the pool, or break them. And even if none of those things happen, they'll probably be out of fashion by next summer. Save your bucks with some drugstore dupes!

3. Accessories.

THIS. What's in style for accessories changes so quickly. In just my lifetime, trends have included HUGE sunglasses, butterfly hair clips, fake lip rings, oversize hair bows, aviator glasses, striped fedora hats, wallets chained to pants, and clear-plastic backpacks. Save your dollars here by avoiding flash-in-the-pan trends.

4. Swimsuits.

This may seem counterintuitive, because you should always OWN a bathing suit. But swimsuit styles change every season, people gain and lose a lot of weight over colder seasons, and you will probably only use it a handful of times per summer. So unless you're thinking of channeling your inner Michael Phelps, save your bucks.

5. Hosiery & socks.

Run, run, run. Any pair of tights or nylons is bound to end up with a run in it. I have torn tights in countless ways, from getting too excited during an impromptu dance move to my ring getting caught on the seam, even from the rough patches on my feet! You'll end up way more disappointed if an expensive pair rips than when an inexpensive pair from a drugstore does. And socks . . . eh, just buy them in a pack. You'll lose half in the dryer anyway.

6. Lingerie.

Unless it lends itself to your profession, you'll probably only wear this a handful of times . . . and likely only for a few minutes (wink, wink!). Costly lingerie is not a smart investment.

7. Jewelry.

You might wear your wedding rings or other family heirlooms regularly, but trends for jewelry change faster than the plot on a soap opera. Unless you're buying an "occasion" piece or a special gift, keep your budget low for earrings, bangles, statement necklaces, and rings. They'll be out of style soon.

8. Athletic gear.

You'll sweat, stretch, stain, and wear through these clothes fast. And if you work out frequently, you probably need a few pairs. No need to drop big money on a single pair of leggings or a T-shirt.

9. Dresses & skirts.

Length, color, and style fluctuate from season to season and year to year. So it's just not worth investing a lot in them.

10. Seasonal stuff.

Halloween costumes, ugly holiday sweaters, tacky Fourth of July swimsuits, and "Kiss Me, I'm Irish" tees are places where you should definitely save your pennies. Honestly, my mom has been wearing the same Statue of Liberty costume since I was a kid. You'll wear seasonal stuff once, maybe twice, in an entire year. Keep your holiday spirit in your pocket.

DOING IT FOR THE 'GRAM

I WAS LATE SIGNING UP FOR INSTAGRAM. Despite making my living in social media, I have always been the last one to snag my handles for new social media platforms. Don't get me wrong, I love social media. It's brought me so much, but I'm still slow to sign up. Chalk it up to sheer laziness.

I downloaded Instagram the summer after my junior year of college, and used it socially until after I was out of college a year later. After I graduated, I started my new job at the theatre, which had full-length mirrors in the dance studio. I would take ten minutes every morning and snap a picture of my outfit.

Until that job, I hadn't cared about my clothes in the slightest. It didn't matter to me. I didn't own a skirt and had one cheap dress that I wore to every job interview, my college graduation, a baby shower, and in a play. It was a completely novel idea to wear "outfits" that were planned with accessories and were a whole *look* in my style.

I started posting my outfit pictures. I never imagined myself to be a #OOTD type of person. That wasn't me. I didn't imagine myself as a fashion maven. I was someone who was discovering for the first time that I was no longer relegated to the frumpy, shapeless, out-of-style sacks that I was able to find in the local surplus store. More and more websites were popping up with extended size options, and more important, I was learning how to find them. I was learning how to dress myself for the first time, at age twenty-two.

I posted every day and used every hashtag I could think of. After a year and a half, I was resting at around 700 followers. Then, I lost my job at the theatre. Within a few weeks of dedicating my time, I had more than doubled my Instagram followers to 1,500. Within a year of that, I was at around 11K; a year after that, 32K, then 50K, then 84K, and now who knows what?! I have connected with incredibly awesome people, heard some unbelievable stories, and challenged myself every day.

When I decided to meet with the Wilsons and not go back to my day job at the university, I knew I could do it. I was smart and savvy and not scared of living within a tight budget. I was trial-ing and error-ing left and right to figure out the best method to connect with brands.

The very first paid #AD was for a woman-owned company called Undersummers. It didn't pay enough to cover even one bill, but for me, I might as well have won the dang lottery. I looked at those dollars and cried. Someone had believed in me enough to take a chance, and that moment made me decide I wanted to chase that feeling more.

A full year later, I had worked with a handful of random brands, connected with some other amazing influencers who have continued to change my life, and, most important, learned so much about making engaging content. I was asking questions, hustling, and trying everything I could think of. I bought my URL.

In the second year, I started figuring out the "industry" side of things. I found platforms to connect with brands, and worked with amazing woman-owned, Black-owned, small, and local shops, and even with a few national brands whose mission statements I believed in. I bought my camera and switched away from old phone photography (this was before they were better than most cameras). I figured out how to pose. I switched all of my social handles.

And here I am, a few years later, and I can't believe how much the industry has grown. I'm constantly amazed by the friends I meet, the stories people share, the brand managers with vision, the creative photographers and artists, and the opportunities I've been allotted.

I constantly get asked about how I grew my social media to the point where it became my career. That's such a broad question, because there wasn't any one thing that led to me being able to take a hobby to a professional level. It was a bunch of things, mixed with good timing and good luck. If you're looking to grow your blog, vlog, video, or influencer page, here are some of the things that would have saved me a ton of time in the trial-and-error department.

1. Pick a "thing."

Now, this may sound silly, but you have to pick a thing. Fashion, beauty, lifestyle, parenting, DIY, craft, sales—whatever it is, commit to it! No one is your exact personality duplicate, so your feed can't be ALL of your interests. I'm a die-hard theatre fan, a bad movie fanatic, a true crime Murderino, a mental health advocate, a lover of dogs and travel, and a million other things. But if my whole feed was mixed up with all those things, no one (except friends and fam) would know my style, which is what I wanted to focus on. Pick a lane (mine is mostly lifestyle) and stick to it!

2. Show me the moneymaker!

Show your face! I know this is super weird, but it's how you let people get to know you. That's what makes people want to follow you in the first place.

3. Quality check.

This is something people are hard-pressed to figure out. You have to post the same type of content every day (sometimes more than once), and usually around the same time of day.

And you don't have to have fancy cameras or lighting to get a good photo. Low-light selfies that clearly have makeup on the lens and outfit photos in dirty full-length mirrors are not high-quality content. Just wipe the lens and the mirror and check out how to get the best light. Making these small adjustments will end up paying off big.

You don't need to have anything fancy to create quality content. You just need to have a good eye for lighting, poses, and angles. It's super easy! Grab a friend and your phone one day and try it out.

4. Aesthetic dreamboat.

You've probably heard the phrase "Your insta aesthetic is lit." What the word "aesthetic" usually refers to is overall content, style, and visual similarity in all your in-feed images. Creating a consistent visual similarity in images and content can help create a brand and drive your content forward.

To edit your aesthetic, you need to figure out your "thing," decide what editing tools and techniques you love, and see which filters suit you. And you don't need anything fancy to edit photos! I use different apps to enhance colors, edit people out of the background, and more.

5. Make 'em laugh.

Okay. This is the easiest trick in the book and no one ever believes me until they try it.

Laugh when someone says smile. Nothing needs to be funny. You don't need to hear a joke or anything. Just make the action of laughing. I swear it works. It gives you a natural smile, and makes your photos look less posed and stiff and awkward.

For real, I love to go up to people who are struggling to take a selfie and ask if they want me to take a picture of them. I usually say, "One two three, smile, one two three, another for good measure, one two three, laugh like you're in an Olive Garden commercial and you clearly just discovered breadsticks," and that usually gets people to chuckle.

And nine times out of ten, that's the photo they end up choosing.

6. Half-price apps.

Okay, maybe the "apps" in "half-price apps" refers to appetizers and not to useful apps for editing, but who can say for sure. Use apps. I edit all my photos, compose all my short-form videos, research popular hashtags, connect with brands, and even keep my budgets all on smartphone apps. Figure out which apps work for you, and then decide which caliber of the app you need. I'm about fifty-fifty on whether I need the paid version or the lite version. Read the reviews and try out the features before you buy!

7. Stay on brand.

There are so many platforms to connect brands and influencers through digital marketing brand reps. Basically, these are middlemen between influencers and brands. Finding these platforms has been how I've grown about half my campaign portfolio. Most are free to use and will help you stay up to date on trends and upcoming fads! I also love being able to see what the "standard rates" are to help price myself.

8. Stop putting your hands on your hips.

It almost never looks as nice and natural as you think it does. If you don't know what to do with your hands, here are some ideas: hold a purse, clutch a coffee, put your hands in your pockets, ruffle your hair, blow a kiss, rustle your skirt, play with your hem, let your arms hang by your sides, let your arms rest on a surface.

9. Ask for anything.

There are so many resources on how to become a blogger, on monetizing content, on photograpy, or whatever you can think of on social media platforms, so for the most part, ask and you shall receive. The first time someone asked me how much money I wanted to make for a sponsored Instagram post, I had no idea. I asked an influencer I admired what she was charging, and adjusted accordingly from there. I've reached out to Insta-friends and asked for ways to connect with brands. I've DMed brands all over the world and just asked if we could work together. I've asked for more money for more work. I needed an extra four days to get this book to my editor. In every situation, all I needed to do was ask.

10. Authenticity is authenti-key.

You'll grow when your goal is to connect. I love posting about my dorky husband, fangirling over musicals, and wearing tutus and funky glasses and scrunchies. I drink so much coffee. I am an annoying dog mom. You probably know a lot of that already because I love sharing details about my life. I just am who I am out loud on Insta, and it has continued to reward me. Everyone can smell a phony baloney from a mile away. Just be you.

POTLUCK
ADVICE

I'VE GIVEN YOU JUST ABOUT ALL THE TOOLS I can about wearing the swimsuit or the crop top. I hope I've changed your mind about jiggling tummies and self-conscious moments we need to acknowledge. I hope you have learned one or two things about yourself and your relationship with your body. But there are moments bigger than that. Here are some pieces of advice I wish literally anyone had told me at any point. If I can open your mind or change your ideas about even one of these things, I will feel like it was totally worth it. Advice is my bread and butter. I love giving advice, and someone let me write a book, so I want to make sure I get a few more good ideas in here before I have to get going.

1. Sometimes you have to let your dad make you a grilled cheese sandwich.

My dad is notoriously overprotective and incredibly kind. I'm very fortunate in that regard. He is constantly checking in to see if I need anything: food, money, a ride, advice, help lifting that heavy box to my car, etc. Sometimes he'll slide a twenty into my wallet "for gas." As you get older, it gets harder and harder for some parents to deal with you not really needing them as much. When I visit my parents now, my dad will list every single thing in the kitchen and say he can make it for me. He even offers to make me some cereal. I'm a grown-up. I am, for the most part, totally capable of providing dinner for myself. But every once in a while, I let my dad make me a grilled cheese sandwich because I know it makes us both happy.

2. Sometimes it REALLY isn't about you.

This has been a hard life lesson to learn. I live in a world with a lot of rejection and criticism. When I lost my job, I got so discouraged when I wasn't getting calls for interviews. I had to remember that sometimes it ISN'T about you. The reason someone else gets picked isn't because the interviewer didn't like you or wasn't impressed with you. There was nothing wrong with you at all.

I auditioned for a show a few years ago and nailed the audition, but the role went to another actress. I asked the director what I could have done better. He told me nothing. He said I was great and he was really impressed. He just was looking for someone with a different body type. It had nothing to do with me at all.

I once thought another guy and I were going to kiss. But he rejected my kiss . . . because he was getting over strep throat. Sometimes the reason a person breaks up with you, doesn't hire you, won't kiss you, won't cast you is not about you and has to do with some nebulous other reason. It's important to remember that there is nothing wrong with you.

3. Growing apart from people is always going to suck.

It doesn't get easier as you get older. As you age and go through stages of your life, people will come and go. Your high school friends move away and your college friends move back home. My best friend moved across the country. It doesn't stop hurting to drift apart from some of your closest people. Even if you're not mad at or angry with them, sometimes life just has different plans. It just . . . sucks. But on that same note, appreciate the friends you do have and make sure to nurture those relationships. If they're important, put the effort in.

4. Sometimes in life you have do things that make you feel bad.

Maybe that means auditioning for the same role as a friend, applying for the same job as a friend, eating the last fry, cutting someone off in traffic because you have to get to the off-ramp and the next exit is twenty miles away, or having to miss someone's event. Maybe you can't find a recycling can. Maybe you don't have time to clean the bathroom before company comes over. It's okay. It does not make you a bad person. The fact that you think it's a bad thing is proof that you aren't a bad person at all.

5. Don't turn down life experiences.

Never turn anything down. Ever. Do a shot, draw a tattoo on your leg and don't wash it off, try a new meal, kiss a person you wouldn't normally kiss, make an online dating profile, take a class you want to take, play a role you hate in a show you don't like, go to a party even though you're tired, drive your friend's car, go to an amateur stand-up comedy night, go to a football game, audition for the musical, watch a movie you've never heard of—just let life happen. As long as you're being safe, responsible, and respectful, you should always agree to things, even if you're feeling like a chicken.

6. You should always have a bathing suit.

You should keep a bathing suit in your car, dorm, college apartment, purse, overnight bag—somewhere it is readily accessible. I literally keep one in my car at all times. Let me tell you why. A bathing suit is an article of clothing that is very difficult to fake and difficult to buy off season on short notice. For example, say you're staying at a friend's house overnight and the two of you make a last-minute decision to go somewhere nice for dinner. If you're not dressed fancy enough, it's easy to go to the mall and grab a nicer top and some accessories fairly inexpensively. If that same friend is having a hot tub party in January, you're in trouble. You should always be prepared for life to take you on an adventure.

7. Your car should always have these five things:

A TOWEL. For bathing suit adventures. For unexpected rainstorms. For accidentally leaving your windows cracked. For drying off the car. Wiping away snow. Having to take a shower at a friend's house unexpectedly. Finding a stray kitten. Wiping grease off your hands. Making a tourniquet. Spreading on the grass as a makeshift picnic blanket. Millions of reasons. You'll never regret having a towel.

BOTTLED WATER. Just in case. In case your car breaks down. In case it's scorching hot. In case something gets on your windshield. In case you have your dog with you and it needs water after an impromptu hike. In case you're thirsty. In case of an emergency. Just . . . in case.

DUCT TAPE. You can pretty much fix anything on your car in a pinch with duct tape. Yeah, you'll look less than pretty with your bumper duct-taped on, but it will at least get you home. There are literally a dozen things duct tape is practical for.

AN INDEX CARD WITH IMPORTANT PHONE NUMBERS. In this day and age, no one memorizes numbers. And if your car breaks down and your phone is dead, or you have no service and have to use a stranger's phone, or you lose your phone, or your purse gets stolen, etc., well, you'll need to call someone. And having recently been in this position myself—you will have no way to call them. You should have a card with any number you might need: AAA, your mom, your boyfriend, your boyfriend's mom, your dad, a few good friends who live in a few places, a local towing company, the local police nonemergency line, etc.

A FEW BUCKS IN CASH. Again, in case you run out of gas, have to get towed, end up on a toll road, have to pay mileage on your car, encounter a cash-only gas station, etc. It's always helpful to have a few emergency dollars tucked into one of the console compartments.

8. It's okay to cry about it.

Mourn your losses. Wallow in your sadness. Embrace it. Eat junk food for three days and don't put on pants. Grieve for stupid things. Important things. Grieve for yourself, because often no one else will. And acknowledging the pain is sometimes the best way to move on. That's why RuPaul invented Ben & Jerry's, *The Notebook*, and the Forever Lazy.*

*Not a fact, but it should be.

9. Stop tolerating bad people.

I recently learned that there are some adults my parents' age in my life whom I do not respect. I've tolerated them. I let them speak to me and my loved ones inappropriately . . . for years. Because at the time, they were an adult and I was a child. But I'm an adult now, too. I don't owe respect to anyone who hasn't done something to earn it. You can be civil or polite. But respect yourself first. Toxicity is never acceptable.

10. Cursing is not the end of the world.

You SHOULD have better vocabulary. You should have other words to use instead of swearing. Yes, I know. I did incredibly well in English class my whole life. But when you bang your toe on the nightstand, a "gee willikers, that smarts" is absolutely NOT a fun substitute for "motherfucker."

11. Know your own limits.

If you're the kind of person who gets ragingly, violently, and aggressively angry when you get jealous, then know the warning signs so you can excuse yourself from the situation. Know how many shots you can take before you puke or pass out. Know the limits of your sexual comfort zone so you can consent or not consent to taking things further with a new or existing partner. Know if you're capable of caring for a dog or if you're more of a cactus person. Try to increase your self-awareness as you grow as a person.

12. Your parents will adjust to the boundaries you set.

You can set boundaries with your parents at any point. They'll adjust to them. You just need to communicate clearly and openly what those limits are and what your expectations are. If you don't tell them, they can't know and respect your boundaries.

13. Stay weird.

You're never too old to wear a goofy Halloween costume, to roll around in Heelys, to watch Saturday-morning cartoons, or to rock cupcake-print pajama pants. You can still have slumber parties with your bestie and totally shine-osaur in a dinosaur dress. Make silly faces, dance in the grocery store, speak in accents when you're passing through a small town, rent a car for a day just to see what it's like to drive something different, spend a commute to work making "car noises" with your mouth, or take a bubble bath. Wear a cape one day. Stay weird as long as humanly possible.

14. Choose your battles.

Otherwise, your whole life will be a string of uphill journeys. Fight for what matters and what counts, and let the rest go.

15. Appreciate the things you take for granted.

And I don't mean the "stop and smell the roses" kind of taking things for granted. I mean indoor plumbing and toilet paper, modern medicine and vaccinations, the internet, free education for ALL young people (no matter their gender, race, socioeconomic standing, or academic prowess), modern sanitation, deodorant and soap, the relative variety of modern clothing, etc.

16. Always ask to pet someone else's dog.

Some dogs bite. Some dogs have fleas. Some dogs are service dogs. Some dogs are service dogs in training. Some dogs are rescue pets with some level of PTSD. Ask first. Most people will say yes, but you always need to ask before petting a dog that isn't yours.

17. Don't snort Pixy Stix.

My eighth-grade self learned this lesson the hard way at the community pool one summer so you don't have to. You're welcome.

18. Having basic kitchen skills is a MUST.

You should be able to make eggs at least three ways, make pasta, and throw together a salad that's not out of a bag. You should know how to make cookies from scratch, a dish or two that're good for potlucks, a basic chip dip, and how to properly cook chicken. If you can make even a few standard dishes, it'll save you a ton of money, time, and calories.

19. When you're moving, pack your books in your rolling suitcases.

Books are heavy. Being able to just roll them out and lift them into the car/truck, then roll them into your new place . . . well, you're going to save some backs from strain. You needed to move your suitcases anyway. Kill two birds with one stone.

20. Life doesn't always take you where you think it will.

If you had asked me a few years ago if I thought the blog I started on a whim would blossom into a huge career thing that would give me both a book deal and travel opportunities, I wouldn't have believed you. I needed a hobby, and that's what brought me to all the lovely people I get to connect with all over the world!

21. On the same note, let it.

You'll discover all the places life can take you if you just let things go where they may. Adventures are seldom born out of ten-year plans.

22. Why bother folding your underwear?

No one cares if they're wrinkled. Everyone knows it's more efficient to roll them so you can see them all. If they're folded, then you can only get the one off the top. It's a waste of time.

23. Know your limits.

A little personal story here. A friend of mine admitted that they were in an abusive relationship. I wanted nothing but to help them, but I couldn't handle it alone. I didn't know what to do or even what I *could* do alone. I confided in another really close mutual friend and we made a plan. As a team, we were able to offer more support and options to get our friend out of their situation. But I knew I needed help to do that. Know when to ask for help.

24. You'll never forget your first big purchase.

Preston and I bought couches and a vacuum recently. The year before, we bought a bed. It's slightly thrilling to actually own big things. Is that dumb? But every time I look at our furniture, I'm so happy. We made a commitment to buy and even pay off things to build a home together. Make those big purchases.

25. "Please" & "thank you" are ageless.

You should say thank you to the stranger who opens the door for you, say please when you order a glass of water, and always remember your manners. No one is ever mad at the really polite person.

26. Change your damn oil.

It's, like, the easiest maintenance for your car. It costs, like, $40. It takes an hour and can literally save you thousands of dollars. I know people who never get their oil changed. Just do it. Please. Please. Please. Change your damn oil. Don't wait for the light to come on. It's the easiest thing you can do to maintain your car.

27. You'll never regret being nice.

You'll never regret not starting a fight, not baiting a jerkwad, complimenting a stranger, letting something small slide even though your day has sucked so far, or holding the door for someone. You won't regret buying the person behind you a cup of coffee or offering to return a cart for a mom who is struggling to get two toddlers into the car at the grocery store.

28. Keep learning.

Learn life lessons. If you are reading this, then you have access to the internet. You can learn sign language, how to cook, what the top ten signs of a toxic relationship are, geometry, how to sew, what pizza topping you are, how to use Excel, or what Myanmar's political climate is like. No excuses. You have access to the internet. But also, read the free newspapers in coffee shops, borrow books from the library, ask your elders. You should always strive to keep learning.

Acknowledgments

THANK YOU to my wonderful husband, Preston. When I say that none of this could be possible without him, it is the biggest understatement in this book. Thank you for literally everything. There aren't enough thank-yous in enough languages.

Thank you to my editor, Ronnie, for knowing I needed every email to start with "Stay calm, everything is going to be fine," because it always was.

They say it takes a village, and I need to thank the amazing Simon & Schuster and Tiller Press village that

Time to reflect

made this possible: Ronnie, Ivy, Patrick, Matt, Laura, Laura, Molly, and, of course, Richard for all the hard work they put in to making this all possible!

Another big thank-you to my second village: the team at Source Creative House. Thank you to Emil, Steph, and Landon for absolutely everything. Couldn't have done it without you. Thank you to additional SCH villagers: Emma, Alanis, and Ivana with MKUP Studio.

Thank you to the friends who listened to me read paragraphs over the phone, edited last-minute, and pitched ideas: Cassie, Hannah, Afa, Justin, Abby, Alex, Bethany, Bricker, and Patrick.

Thank you to my parents, Adam, Rachel, and Emmett. I feel like thanking Preston a second time is totally worth it. Thanks, honey. You're simply the best.

About the Author

ABBY HOY is a body-positive and colorful lifestyle content creator and influencer. She spends her time being weird in Pennsylvania with her husband, Preston, and her beloved rescue morkie, Charlie.